COUNTRY ENTERTAINING

COUNTRY ENTERTAINING

JOANNA SHEEN

Photography by Debbie Patterson

CHARLES LETTS · Letts · FOUNDED 1796 ·

I would like to dedicate this book to my mother, Diana Hatherly.
She taught me all the basics of cookery and entertaining,
and then showed me, by example, how to create a happy family occasion
that is still remembered long after it is over. Thank you for
giving me so much and asking for so little

First published in 1991
by Charles Letts & Co Ltd
Diary House, Borough Road
London SE1 1DW

ISBN 1 85238 163 9

A CIP catalogue record for this book is available from the British Library.

'Letts' is a registered trademark of Charles Letts (Scotland) Ltd

Project editor: Jane Struthers
Designers: Peartree Design Associates
Home economist: Meg Jansz
Illustrator: Hussein Hussein
Typeset by Central Southern Typesetters, Eastbourne
Colour production by Daylight Colour Art Pte. Ltd
Printed and bound in Hong Kong

Important: Use only one set of measurements. The quantities given in metric
are not always exact conversions of the imperial measurements.

The quantities given in this book err on the generous side, because there's
nothing I hate more than following a recipe that claims to feed four yet
barely produces enough food for two!

CONTENTS

INTRODUCTION

As I sit writing this, looking out of the window, there are dozens of sheep with their lambs dashing past giving a very good impression of organized chaos. The sheep live in two fields, one each end of the village, so they have to pass through the village fairly regularly when they change fields. In many ways there is little to choose between this chaotic herd of sheep and the traffic during the rush hour; both are noisy and apparently chaotic but they reach their destinations eventually.

The big difference as far as I'm concerned is that it is a joy to sit and watch these animals, particularly the lambs. In between yelling for their mothers, they suddenly find a stone or stick that they decide must be regarded with suspicion and so leap into the air and rush on. The countryside has so much to offer if you have the time to appreciate it. One of the most enjoyable aspects of moving to the country for me was being able to entertain my friends and family and to be able to share the surrounding views and special places.

London, New York, Los Angeles, Sydney, Tokyo or whichever town or city you care to mention has a tremendous number of attractions. I have to admit our choice of cultural venues is limited in the village, but there are many other benefits that towns can never even begin to compete with. Although I regularly visit large cities all over the world, I am always very glad to come home. My heart still skips a beat when I first see the sea and I will always consider it a privilege to live in such congenial and lovely surroundings.

Of course there is more to the country than just the beautiful views; it has also come to represent traditional values and the sort of products that take time rather than money. There is nothing more relaxing than a weekend spent with good friends taking long country walks and enjoying good country food. It is difficult to say what country food really is, but I would describe it as being made from fresh, good quality ingredients, cooked with a little TLC (tender loving care). That does not mean that it has to be dull, unimaginative or based on recipes that have been popular for many years. The countryside is always changing and renewing itself and so our cookery moves on.

There will always be a place for family recipes that have given pleasure over many years, and indeed I have often found inspiration in Roman or medieval cookery books. But with the arrival of new ingredients that have not always been readily available in times gone by, so our recipes have changed and altered accordingly. Many of the recipes in this book have been made up due to last-minute problems; perhaps something I wanted to use was not ripe enough or even available. Another common problem that has been a creative catalyst is a glut of some ingredient or other. Often tomatoes or apples, cucumbers or marrows, are around in such huge quantities that when you offer some to a neighbour you hear a groan rather than a thank you. This is the time for cooks to rise to the challenge and see whether they can use the glut of produce in such a way that the family don't say, 'Oh no, not tomatoes again' at the next meal.

I have included many recipes in this book that are old family standbys, because they are the basis upon which I started cooking and many of them were just too good to leave out. Our family has always enjoyed entertaining, and even if a dreadful feeling of 'Why did I get myself into this' creeps over me at the last minute, by the time everyone has arrived I always begin to enjoy myself. The most important rule is to relax; your friends or family have come to see *you* and if they are going to make too much of a fuss over the standard of the food, then shame on them!

'If in doubt, pick the easy way out', is a phrase I would highly recommend when it comes to food and cookery in general. If a special occasion is looming on the horizon and you have the choice between cooking an easy meal that you feel confident about or a complicated alternative that includes a lot of recipes that are new to you, I would strongly suggest you choose the former option. Just because a meal is incredibly complicated to cook does not mean it will be incredibly successful. I have often eaten at good restaurants and wished that some of the food could have been plainer instead of covered with three sauces or made into umpteen different shapes. In contrast, we have eaten simple meals with friends that rely heavily on good local ingredients and basic cooking techniques, and which we have remembered for years.

Food may be the centrepiece of your entertainment but it is only part of the story. Flowers to decorate the house or table make an enormous contribution and little extras placed around the house, such as your own brand of pot-pourri or lavender sachets in the drawers, add an extra dimension to your guests' enjoyment. It doesn't matter whether you are entertaining in central London or in deepest Scotland, you can still adopt the feel of the countryside and the caring attitude of its inhabitants.

I hope you will enjoy trying out all these recipes and that they may make a small contribution towards the success of a special occasion, whether it is a large and grand event or a simple everyday meal.

JOANNA SHEEN

COUNTRY BREAKFASTS

Breakfast during the week is often a very hurried meal, with everyone grabbing their particular breakfast choice while keeping one eye on the clock. All the more reason, then, to relax at weekends and take a little longer over the first meal of the day. I'm not really at my best when we have breakfast very early during the week (I'm barely awake), but a weekend brunch or late breakfast is a meal I really enjoy. Guests are usually relaxed and if it is warm and sunny, everyone is in a good mood and looking forward to a fun day with friends or family.

The easiest way to produce an extra special breakfast is to organize everything the night before. I know that in my case it's no good leaving everything to the last minute, otherwise it never happens. If mornings aren't your strong point then be kind to yourself: make sure everything is waiting in the fridge and that you only have to put the last-minute ingredients together.

An extravagant table decoration would be quite out of keeping, but it only takes a couple of minutes to rush into the garden, pick a few fresh flowers and put them in a small vase. All you need are a few daffodils, roses or other flowers to create a pretty table.

Some decorations can be planned in advance for special occasions. At Easter, for instance, you could make tiny nests containing little eggs, either blown quail's eggs or small chocolate ones. For Christmas, perhaps you could make small hessian sacks with gold coins spilling out of them and a mouse or hedgehog made from a teazel head.

If you are prepared to make an early start, why not plan a breakfast party on a Sunday for friends or family instead of having them to lunch? It makes a great change and all the adults can dive into the Sunday papers while the children rush around creating total mayhem and having a good time. If you're feeling weak at the very thought of entertaining anyone on a Sunday morning, maybe you could follow one or two of the recipe ideas to cook breakfast for two, which you can eat in total silence until the aspirins start to work!

ABOVE RIGHT: SAGE COMES IN A VARIETY OF DIFFERENT FORMS, BUT I LOVE SEEING POTS OF THIS 'TRICOLOR' SAGE. BELOW: THESE JUGS OF FLOWERS AND FOLIAGE WOULD MAKE A LOVELY INFORMAL DISPLAY FOR A LARGE BREAKFAST TABLE.

APRICOT AND PEACH MUESLI

This muesli is amazingly delicious and not what we have come to expect from muesli at all. It takes some time to make, which may rule it out as an everyday breakfast idea, but it is yummy for weekends or special occasions.

120 g (8 tbsp) oats (or mixed cereals)	1 small melon
350 ml (12 fl oz) water	4 fresh peaches (can be tinned in desperation)
30 g (2 tbsp) chopped hazelnuts	6 fresh apricots (can be tinned in desperation)
30 g (2 tbsp) chopped blanched almonds	8 strawberries for decoration (optional)
100 ml (4 fl oz) double cream	

———— SERVES 8 ————

Soak the oats overnight in the water. The following morning, mix in the nuts and the double cream. Finely chop the melon and fresh apricots and add to the mixture. Divide between 8 bowls. Peel and slice the fresh peaches and mix with each bowl's contents. Finally, decorate each bowl with a whole strawberry if you wish.

PORK AND HERB PATTIES WITH STUFFED TOMATOES

These patties are relatively simple to make and I find they are always very popular. They can be made in advance.

750 g (1 lb 11 oz) minced pork	50 g (2 oz) long-grain rice
75 g (3 oz) granary breadcrumbs	25 g (1 oz) sultanas
1 medium-sized dessert apple	30 ml (2 tbsp) apple chutney
1 onion	4 fresh sage leaves
pinch of mixed herbs	2 or 3 sprigs of fresh thyme
8 small tomatoes	parsley for decoration

━━━━━ SERVES 8 ━━━━━

Boil the long-grain rice, following the manufacturer's instructions, until tender. While it is still hot, mix in the sultanas, apple chutney and very finely chopped fresh sage and thyme. Slice a lid off each tomato and, using a small melon baller, scoop out the contents and discard. Fill the tomatoes with the rice mixture and replace the lids.

Peel, core and grate the dessert apple. Peel and chop finely the onion. Mix together the minced pork, apple, breadcrumbs, mixed herbs and onion. Make 8 patties and place under a hot grill until cooked through. The tomatoes can be put on a baking sheet and warmed through in the oven just before serving the patties. Garnish with parsley.

MUESLI YOU HAVE MADE YOURSELF WITH FRESH FRUIT AND SERVED WITH CREAM IS A WONDERFUL INDULGENCE AND A COMPLETELY DIFFERENT EXPERIENCE FROM EATING THE PACKET VARIETY.

SCRAMBLED EGG AND SMOKED SALMON IN DILL FILO PASTRIES

Rumour has it that Prince Charles likes scrambled eggs and smoked salmon for breakfast; I'm sure in that case that he would love this version. Anyway, even if he doesn't, Adrian, my husband, loves this combination so that is recommendation in itself! You could also use this recipe as a light lunch dish and serve it with salad.

GUESTS STAYING WITH US FOR THE WEEKEND ARE ALWAYS VERY IMPRESSED WHEN I SERVE SCRAMBLED EGG AND SMOKED SALMON IN DILL FILO PASTRIES. EVEN IF THEY SAY THEY DON'T EAT BREAKFAST, THEY ALWAYS SEEM TO CHANGE THEIR MINDS WHEN THIS DISH IS MENTIONED!

8 large free-range eggs (yes, you can taste the difference!)	salt and black pepper
	25-50 g (1-2 oz) fresh dill
75-100 g (3-4 oz) smoked salmon	350 g (12 oz) filo pastry
	225 g (8 oz) butter
225 g (8 oz) cream cheese	miniature tomatoes or parsley for decoration
200 ml (8 tbsp) milk	
25 g (1 oz) butter	

SERVES ABOUT 8

Chop the smoked salmon, some of the dill (the exact quantity depends on your taste) and mix these two ingredients with the cream cheese. Add a pinch of salt and a liberal sprinkling of freshly milled black pepper. Melt the 225 g (8 oz) of butter in a pan. Take a sheet of filo pastry and butter it with a brush. Fold it in half and put about an eighth of the salmon and cream cheese mixture on top of the sheet of pastry. Fold over as shown in the diagram. Once all the triangles have been prepared, place them on a baking sheet and brush the tops with butter. Bake in a pre-heated oven at 200°C (400°F), Gas Mark 6, for about 20 minutes until they are golden.

Meanwhile, break the eggs into a medium-sized bowl and add the milk, a pinch of salt and some pepper. Beat well with a fork. Just before you serve the dish, melt the 25 g (1 oz) of butter in a pan and pour in the egg mixture. Cook gently, stirring constantly,

but do not overcook. Serve a triangle of salmon filo with some scrambled egg and decorate with tiny tomatoes or parsley.

COURGETTE MUFFINS WITH ORANGE HONEY

I'm not very keen on eating a full cooked breakfast but these muffins certainly go down brilliantly.

225 g (8 oz) wholemeal flour	1 large egg
2 g (½ tsp) baking powder	100 ml (4 fl oz) grapeseed or sunflower oil
2 g (½ tsp) baking soda	1 large courgette
2 g (½ tsp) salt	75 g (3 oz) sultanas
2 g (½ tsp) ground allspice	75 g (3 oz) chopped walnuts
250 g (9 oz) demerara sugar	
ORANGE HONEY CHEESE	
225 g (8 oz) cream cheese	zest of one orange
15 ml (1 tbsp) orange juice	15 ml (1 tbsp) runny honey

MAKES ABOUT 12

Sift together the flour, baking powder, baking soda, salt and allspice. In a separate bowl, combine the sugar and egg and beat well until light and creamy. Add the oil and beat for another 2 or 3 minutes. Grate the courgette finely and add to the egg, sugar and oil mixture. Stir in the sultanas and walnuts, then gently fold in the dry ingredients but do not mix too heavily. Spoon the mixture into greased muffin tins. Bake in a pre-heated oven at 180°C (350°F), Gas Mark 4, for 25-30 minutes until lightly brown. Turn out and cool on a wire rack.

Serve with Orange Honey Cheese (see below).

Orange Honey Cheese
Whip all the ingredients together until light and fluffy, then refrigerate until required.

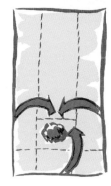

I ONLY EVER BUY EGGS THAT ARE FREE-RANGE THESE DAYS: THEY HAVE A MUCH BETTER FLAVOUR THAN THEIR BATTERY-HEN COUNTERPARTS.

THIS DIAGRAM SHOWS HOW TO FOLD UP THE FILO PASTRY TO MAKE THE TRIANGLES.

BANANA AND BLUEBERRY MUFFINS WITH ALMONDS

I really enjoy cooked bananas; the cooking seems to bring out their taste even more than eating them raw. A basket of assorted muffins looks very attractive on the breakfast table, so make a batch of each sort.

2 large eggs	175 g (6 oz) blueberries
50 ml (2 fl oz) sunflower oil	225 g (8 oz) flour
175 ml (6 fl oz) milk	10 g (2 tsp) baking powder
50 ml (2 oz) honey	2 g (½ tsp) salt
1 large banana, mashed	100 g (4 oz) flaked almonds

━━━━━ MAKES ABOUT 12 ━━━━━

Remove any stalks from the blueberries and mash them with the banana. Beat together the eggs, oil, milk and honey until light and creamy, then add the banana and blueberries. Sieve in the salt, flour and baking powder, add the almonds and fold in gently. Spoon the mixture into greased muffin tins. Bake in a pre-heated oven at 180°C (350°F), Gas Mark 4, for 20-25 minutes until lightly brown. Turn out and cool on a wire rack.

PINK GRAPEFRUIT AND GINGER MARMALADE

Making marmalade is a fairly time-consuming job, but you really can taste the difference between a good home-made marmalade and one bought from a supermarket. At least this recipe can be made in advance and stored until needed (if you have enough willpower).

2 kg (4 lb) small pink grapefruit	30 ml (2 tbsp) orange juice
30 g (2 tbsp) finely chopped stem ginger	30 ml (2 tbsp) lemon juice
3 kg (6 lb 12 oz) preserving sugar	

MAKES 2.4 KG (5½ LB)

Scrub the grapefruit well to remove any chemicals that have been sprayed on the skins. Place them in a large saucepan and cover with water. Simmer gently for about 1-2 hours until they feel soft, then strain and reserve the liquid. Cut up the grapefruit and peel into small pieces, and tie the pips into a small muslin bag. Add the orange and lemon juice to the remaining cooking liquid and, if necessary, top it up to 2.4 litres (4 pints) with cold water.

Place the liquid, grapefruit pieces, pip bag and sugar in a preserving pan and very gently heat until the sugar dissolves. Then bring to the boil and boil rapidly until setting point is reached. (If you are using a thermometer, setting point is at 221°F [105°C]. If not, spoon a little marmalade on to a chilled saucer, allow to cool and then push your finger across its surface – it will wrinkle when it has reached setting point.) Have some warm, clean jars waiting. Chop the stem ginger very finely and stir it into the mixture, then remove the pip bag. Ladle into the jars, cover and seal immediately.

THE TASTE OF HOME-MADE MARMALADE MORE THAN MAKES UP FOR THE EFFORT INVOLVED IN MAKING IT. IF YOU MADE A DOUBLE BATCH OF THE PINK GRAPEFRUIT AND GINGER MARMALADE YOU COULD GIVE SOME OF IT AWAY FOR CHRISTMAS OR BIRTHDAY PRESENTS.

PICNICS

In our English climate it is important to grab any summer sunshine that comes along and to make the most of the lovely warm weekends when they happen. If you are lucky enough to live in a constantly warm climate then picnics can happen more often than they do here.

Eating out of doors is much more exciting, and often appetites are larger than they would be if the same food were laid out on the dining room table at home. Planning a large outdoor event can be fun when several families get together; that way you can all help with the cooking and no one is over-worked.

Remember to pack plenty of napkins and damp cloths to wipe sticky faces and fingers (even if there aren't any children on this picnic) and comfortable rugs or blankets to sit on. Traditional picnic hampers look wonderful and add real style to a picnic, but you can have just as much fun with an odd assortment of shopping bags, baskets and paper plates. An occasion is what you make of it and the company is just as important as the food, so don't worry if you can't produce a picnic feast on a scale to rival the most lavish Victorian outing.

CHILLED CUCUMBER AND AVOCADO SOUP

Here is another of my absolutely favourite recipes. I love avocados anyway, and this creamy soup is delicious.

2-3 ripe avocados, depending on size	60 ml (4 tbsp) lime juice
½ large cucumber	salt and black pepper
300 ml (½ pint) sour cream or Greek yoghurt	5 g (1 tsp) minced garlic
	5 g (1 tsp) chilli powder
600 ml (1 pint) chicken or vegetable stock	

SERVES ABOUT 8

Peel the avocados and place in a food processor or blender with the cucumber, roughly chopped. Process until smooth. Turn into a large mixing bowl and add all the other ingredients. Taste and adjust the seasonings accordingly. Chill in the refrigerator for an hour or two before serving. Garnish with slices of cucumber or sprigs of watercress.

TRANSPORTING THE CHILLED CUCUMBER AND AVOCADO SOUP TO THE PICNIC IN A THERMOS FLASK WILL ENSURE IT STAYS COOL.

POTATO AND DILL SALAD
IN GREEK MAYONNAISE

This is easy to make and always very, very popular.

1 kg (2¼ lb) new potatoes	225 ml (8 fl oz) good mayonnaise
50 g (2 oz) finely chopped fresh dill	225 ml (8 fl oz) Greek yoghurt
	salt and black pepper

SERVES 8

Clean the potatoes, then place in a saucepan of cold water and bring to the boil. Cook until tender – about 10 minutes after the water has boiled. While the potatoes are cooking, mix together the yoghurt, dill, mayonnaise, salt and pepper.

When the potatoes are ready, drain them well and place in a mixing bowl. Pour over the mayonnaise mixture and leave to cool. Once the potatoes are cool, refrigerate them for several hours. Before serving, turn the potatoes well in the dressing and decorate with a sprig of dill.

APRICOT AND CASHEW
RICE SALAD

Here is a delicious and versatile recipe that would go well with many different foods. You can vary the ingredients according to what you have available.

225 g (8 oz) dried apricots	100 ml (4 fl oz) white wine vinegar
300 ml (½ pint) white wine	15 g (3 tsp) mixed salt and pepper
275 g (10 oz) uncooked rice	5 g (1 tsp) minced garlic
100 g (4 oz) cashew nuts	30 g (2 tbsp) castor sugar
100 g (4 oz) cooked *petits pois*	225 g (8 oz) minced onion
300 ml (½ pint) virgin olive oil	

SERVES 8

Chop the apricots and place in a bowl. Pour over the white wine and leave to soak for several hours. Cook the rice, then rinse well with cold water to cool. Combine the olive oil, wine vinegar, salt and pepper, garlic, castor sugar and minced onion and whisk together really well.

Mix together the rice, *petits pois*, drained apricots and cashew nuts. Pour on the dressing and toss well. This salad can be made several hours in advance. Before serving, toss it again and decorate with parsley, either chopped or in sprigs.

CHICKEN WINGS IN
ORIENTAL MARINADE

Who says you have to take sandwiches on picnics? These are much more fun but be sure to have lots of wet tissues and towels at the ready to clean up the mess.

12 chicken wings	30 ml (2 tbsp) medium sherry
125 g (4½ oz) brown sugar	
50 ml (2 fl oz) lime juice	2 cloves garlic
	15 ml (1 tbsp) soy sauce
15 g (3 tsp) finely grated fresh ginger root	
	black pepper

SERVES 8

Combine all the ingredients, except the chicken, in a saucepan. Stir over a low heat until all the sugar has dissolved. Bring the sauce to the boil and boil rapidly for 2-3 minutes, then remove from the heat.

Place the chicken wings in a large roasting pan and pour the sauce over them, then leave to marinade for at least 2 hours. Remove the wings from the marinade and transfer to another shallow tin or dish that will hold all the wings. Bake in a pre-heated oven at 200°C (400°F), Gas Mark 6 for about 10 minutes, then baste with more sauce. Bake for another 10 minutes. Then put the wings under the grill for about 5 minutes to crisp them up a little. They can be served hot or cold.

GINGER AND CRANBERRY RIBS

Another messy dish that goes down a storm with all age groups. Both this recipe and the previous one for chicken wings are equally good hot or cold.

8 large pork spare ribs	10 ml (2 tsp) soy sauce
600 ml (1 pint) cranberry juice	15 g (3 tsp) grated fresh ginger root
150 ml (¼ pint) cider vinegar	30 ml (2 tbsp) ginger wine
10 g (2 tsp) cornflour	salt and pepper

SERVES 8

If possible, ask your butcher to chop the ribs in half for you, as this makes them a much better size to cope with when you eat them. If this is not possible, try to chop them in half yourself with a heavy cleaver (mind your fingers), or give up and leave them as large pieces. Place all the ribs in a saucepan, cover with water and add the vinegar. Bring to the boil and boil, uncovered, for 15 minutes. Drain and rinse well, then place in a shallow baking dish.

Mix the cornflour with the soy sauce in a tea cup. Then, in a larger jug or bowl, mix together the cranberry juice, ginger root, ginger wine, salt and pepper, and stir in the soy sauce and cornflour mixture. Pour over the ribs and bake in a pre-heated oven at 170°C (325°F), Gas Mark 3 for approximately an hour. Turn the ribs in the sauce before removing them from the pan and either serve hot or at room temperature.

A SIMPLE SALAD OF SLICED TOMATOES AND FRESH BASIL LEAVES WOULD BE A DELICIOUS AND COLOURFUL ADDITION TO THE PICNIC.

ABOVE: IT NEVER FAILS TO
AMAZE ME WHEN I SEE
PEOPLE PICNICKING ON
THE SIDE OF A
MOTORWAY; THERE ARE
MANY MORE ATTRACTIVE
PLACES TO CHOOSE FROM!

ELDERBERRY CHUTNEY

Here is a lovely rich chutney that is a useful stand-by at any time of year.

450 g (1 lb) elderberries	900 ml (1½ pints) white wine vinegar
1.3 kg (3 lb) apples	
100 g (4 oz) stoned prunes	550 g (1 lb 4 oz) dark brown sugar
50 g (2 oz) sultanas	10 g (2 tsp) ground allspice
50 g (2 oz) stem ginger	90 ml (6 tbsp) ginger wine

—— MAKES ABOUT 1.8 KG (4 LB) ——

Remove the elderberries from their stems, wash them lightly and dry well. Peel and core the apples and chop them into small to medium chunks. Chop the prunes into small chunks. Place all the ingredients in a large pan (not aluminium) and cook until the sugar has dissolved. Bring the mixture to the boil and simmer for about an hour, stirring occasionally, until it has thickened. Have some warm, clean jam jars waiting and pour or ladle the mixture into them. Seal at once with cellophane lids or with clean, non-metallic screw tops. This chutney tastes better if you let it mature for a few weeks before eating it.

FACING PAGE: EASILY
EATEN WITH THE FINGERS,
THESE MINIATURE
CHICKEN AND MUSHROOM
PIES ARE VERY MOREISH
WHEN SERVED WITH
ELDERBERRY CHUTNEY
OR ONION JAM
(see page 25).

MINIATURE CHICKEN AND MUSHROOM PIES

These pies are great favourites with both family and friends. I never bother to make my own puff pastry as the kind you can buy in supermarkets is delicious and saves both time and temper. These beat pork pies hands down.

175 g (6 oz) button mushrooms	15 ml (1 tbsp) sherry
	salt and black pepper
225 g (8 oz) cooked chicken	75 g (3 oz) *petits pois*
75 g (3 oz) butter	1 medium egg
	15 ml (1 tbsp) milk
50 g (2 oz) self-raising flour	450 g (1 lb) puff pastry
225 ml (8 fl oz) good chicken stock	

—— SERVES 8 ——

Using about 25 g (1 oz) of the butter, sauté the sliced mushrooms until just tender. Remove from the heat. Melt the remaining 50 g (2 oz) of butter in the pan, add the flour and cook, stirring all the time, for about 2 minutes. Do not let the butter turn brown. Add the chicken stock, sherry and salt and plenty of freshly milled black pepper. Bring to the boil and simmer gently, stirring constantly, until the sauce is thickened: this will probably take about 2 minutes. Stir in the chicken, mushrooms and *petits pois*.

Roll out half the pastry on a lightly floured board, into a square between 25-30 cm (10-12 in) across. Beat together the egg and milk. Cut the square of pastry into quarters, and brush away any excess flour. Taking one of the pastry squares, brush all four edges with some of the egg and milk mix. Place about one-eighth of the chicken mixture in the centre of the square, then fold it into a triangle and seal the edges between your thumb and forefinger. Place on a greased baking sheet. Make up the other three pastry squares in the same way, then repeat the process with the remaining pastry

and chicken mixture. Brush the tops of the triangles with more of the egg and milk mixture and bake in a pre-heated oven at 190°C (375°F), Gas Mark 5, for 15-20 minutes or until golden brown.

BEEF FILLET WITH APPLE MUSTARD

If you are short of time and have a good delicatessen nearby then buy some ready-cooked and sliced beef for this recipe. Choose some that is slightly rare rather than of the boot-leather variety.

1 kg (2¼ lb) fillet of beef	150 g (5 oz) wholegrain mustard
3 cooking apples	1.2 litres (2 pints) water
15 g (3 tsp) demerara sugar, or to taste	

SERVES ABOUT 8-10

Rinse the fillet of beef and pat dry. Place in a roasting tin and surround with approximately 1.2 litres (2 pints) of water (the exact amount will depend on the size of tin you are using). The water should be about 2.5 cm (1 in) deep. Cook in a pre-heated oven at 200°C (400°F), Gas Mark 6 for about half an hour, depending on how rare you like your beef. Remove from the roasting tin and leave to cool.

Peel, core and chop the apples and place in a pan with barely enough water to cover. Cook gently and lightly, adding the sugar if the apples are quite tart. (If they are sweet, you may not need to add any sugar.) When the apples are just tender, drain well and leave to cool, then mash them with a fork and stir in the mustard.

To serve, slice the beef thinly and spread some of the mustard and apple mixture along the long side of the slice of beef and roll it up. If necessary, hold it in position with cocktail sticks. Serve more of the mustard and apple mixture separately.

JO'S CARROT CAKE

If the proof of the pudding is in the eating then a certain editor, photographer and assistant on this book must have quite liked this recipe! Many people who haven't tried carrot cake before are a little nervous of it, but it really is yummy and doesn't last long. If, however, you do have any left it keeps really well. As a change you could sandwich the cake together with curd cheese instead of double cream.

30 ml (2 tbsp) runny honey	175 g (6 oz) self-raising flour
175 g (6 oz) demerara sugar	300 g (11 oz) grated carrot
225 ml (8 fl oz) grapeseed or sunflower oil	125 g (4½ oz) unsweetened desiccated coconut
3 large eggs	125 g (4½ oz) shelled pecan nuts
5 g (1 tsp) ground allspice	1 × 425 g (15 oz) tin crushed pineapple
pinch of salt	300 ml (½ pint) double cream

SERVES 8

Line the base of a 20 cm (8 in) cake tin with greaseproof paper and grease the base and sides well with butter. Place the oil, sugar and honey in a medium-size mixing bowl and, using an electric mixer or manual whisk, mix for a minute or two until well combined. Add the eggs, one at a time, and whisk until the mixture is light and creamy.

Add the salt and allspice to the flour. Sieve the flour into the bowl, whisking in a little at a time, until it is all incorporated. Stir in the coconut and pecan nuts, then lastly add the grated carrot. Stir again. Pour into the prepared cake tin. Bake in a pre-heated oven at 180°C (350°F), Gas Mark 4 for about 1½ hours. See if the cake is cooked by plunging a knitting needle into its centre – it should come away clean. When the cake is done, remove it from the

oven and turn out on to a wire rack to cool.

Whip the cream and fold in the drained crushed pineapple. Once the cake has cooled, carefully slice it in half horizontally and sandwich it together with the pineapple and cream mixture. The cake should then be kept refrigerated or cool if possible.

CONFITURE D'OIGNONS, OR ONION JAM

This is a slightly more unusual chutney that is a great favourite with onion-lovers.

675 g (1½ lb) onions	175 g (6 oz) sugar
125 g (4½ oz) butter	105 ml (7 tbsp) red wine vinegar
salt and pepper	
	225 ml (8 fl oz) red wine

SERVES 8 AS A RELISH

Peel and slice the onions thinly. Heat the butter in a pan and, once it has melted, cook it for a minute or so but do not let it burn! Add the onions, then add some salt and pepper to taste (I used 5 g [1 tsp] of salt and 7 g [1½ tsp] of black pepper). Stir in the sugar and mix well. Simmer with the lid on for 30-40 minutes, stirring from time to time. As the onions near the end of the cooking time you should take extra care that they don't burn, so keep a watchful eye over them.

Stir in the vinegar and red wine. Cook for another 30 minutes, this time with the lid off, stirring often. Have some warm, clean jam jars waiting and spoon the mixture into them, cover and seal with cellophane circles or screw-top lids. This relish should be stored in the fridge and will keep for at least a month.

DON'T FORGET TO TAKE ALONG A BASKET OF FRUIT – FRESH AIR ALWAYS SEEMS TO GIVE PEOPLE ENORMOUS APPETITES!

WEDDING CELEBRATIONS

These recipes do not have to be used for a wedding; they would be equally useful for any other large gathering, such as a christening, a golden wedding or a retirement party.

Deciding to cater for your own or your daughter's wedding is a brave and ambitious project, but it will bring a tremendous amount of satisfaction when you see all the food laid out on the tables on the day. The main key to it all is organization. Lists and more lists – that's the way I plan everything, even down to the point of making a list of how many lists I have to make! Don't laugh, it works for me! The more organized you are the less likelihood there is of you getting into a major panic, and even if you do it may not last so long. The other key to success is a few extra pairs of hands. Try not to lumber yourself with helpers who cause more trouble than they're worth; what you really need are sensible, calm people who do what you ask and don't come up with wonderful last-minute ideas or try to change everything just when you think you're beginning to see the light at the end of the tunnel.

Make sure you can work with your volunteers; the last thing you want is extra stress in the kitchen. Hiring china, glass and cutlery will solve many problems, but always err on the side of generosity when estimating how much you will need. You can borrow bits and pieces from friends and family, but it's a nightmare trying to remember who has lent what, and embarrassing or acrimonious if you accidentally break something. So if you still think you could organize a big party (and I'm sure you can), you'd better start writing out those lists!

STRIPY LETTUCE

Mixing the colours of the lettuce helps to create a bright patch of colour on the table. If we ever have any leftovers our rabbit thinks this superior form of lettuce is the best, but he's one of those rabbits with expensive tastes!

1 Lollo Rosso lettuce	5 g (1 tsp) black pepper
1 Lollo Blanco lettuce	5 g (1 tsp) sugar
100 ml (4 fl oz) white wine vinegar	2 g (½ tsp) mustard
150 ml (¼ pint) virgin olive oil	½ red pepper
	½ green pepper
5 g (1 tsp) salt	
SERVES 10, SO MAKE 5 BATCHES	

FACING PAGE: LETTUCE CAN BE A VERY DIFFICULT VEGETABLE TO EAT WHEN STANDING UP AND JUGGLING A PLATE, GLASS AND KNIFE AND FORK, NOT TO MENTION MAKING POLITE CONVERSATION, SO BE KIND TO YOUR GUESTS AND CUT THE LETTUCE UP INTO MANAGEABLE PIECES. THIS STRIPY LETTUCE IS EASY TO EAT AND ALSO LOOKS VERY DRAMATIC, ESPECIALLY IF SERVED ON A LARGE WHITE PLATTER.

Combine the wine vinegar, olive oil and seasonings in a food processor and mix together really thoroughly. Pour into a measuring jug. Place the green pepper in the processor and then add half the dressing mixture. Process for about 20 seconds until really well chopped and combined. Put the green dressing to one side. Then put the red pepper and the remainder of the dressing in the processor and again process for about 20 seconds.

Shred the Lollo Rosso lettuce finely, place in a bowl and pour over the red dressing. Toss well and put to one side. Shred the Lollo Blanco lettuce and place in a bowl, pour over the green dressing and toss thoroughly. Choose a flat serving dish and arrange broad, alternate, stripes of red and green lettuce across the plate. You can garnish with some strips or small squares of pepper if you like.

TOMATO AND ORANGE SALAD

You can vary this recipe by using chopped fresh mint and plain cider or red wine vinegar instead of basil vinegar. Experiment and see which combination you prefer.

6 large beefsteak tomatoes	150 ml (¼ pint) olive oil
	5 g (1 tsp) sugar
6 large juicy oranges	5 g (1 tsp) black pepper
100 ml (4 fl oz) basil vinegar (see page 115)	2 g (½ tsp) salt
SERVES 10, SO MAKE 5 BATCHES	

Peel the oranges and separate into segments, taking care to remove all the skin and white pith. Chop them in half. Boil some water in a medium-sized pan (enough to cover at least one large tomato). Make a cross in the skin of each tomato. Place them one at a time in the pan and leave for a few seconds until the skin is loosened. Peel away the skin and then repeat for the next tomato. Slice the tomatoes about 6mm (¼ in) thick and cut the slices in half.

Combine the vinegar, oil and seasonings in a blender and mix together really well. Then put the tomato pieces, oranges and dressing in a bowl and combine thoroughly. Serve garnished with something green, such as sprigs of parsley or watercress.

CARROT, DATE AND PECAN SALAD

I regularly make this salad for lunches during my course weekends. I concocted it when I was searching for a vegetarian option and it was such a success that it has stayed on the menu ever since.

900 g (2 lb) carrots	150 ml (¼ pint) unsweetened orange juice
450 g (1 lb) fresh dates	
225 g (8 oz) pecan nut halves	

— SERVES ABOUT 10, SO MAKE 5 BATCHES —

Peel, top and tail the carrots, then grate them coarsely. Remove the stones and skins from the dates and chop into quarters. Mix together the grated carrot, chopped dates and pecan nuts and pour over the orange juice. Stir well.

This salad can be made a few hours in advance and kept in the fridge until needed, but it won't keep overnight.

LEMON AND MINT CABBAGE SALAD

This is coleslaw with a delicious twist. It always disappears rapidly whenever I produce it.

675 g (1½ lb) white cabbage	15 g (3 tsp) salt
2 green peppers	20 g (4 tsp) castor sugar
4 medium-sized courgettes	20 g (4 tsp) freshly milled black pepper
25 g (1 oz) fresh mint leaves	300 ml (½ pint) grapeseed or sunflower oil
85 ml (3½ fl oz) white wine vinegar	1 lemon
100 ml (4 fl oz) lemon juice	handful of mint sprigs

— SERVES 12, SO MAKE 4 BATCHES —

Grate the cabbage finely, and chop the green peppers and courgettes. In a blender or food processor, chop the fresh mint leaves then add the vinegar, lemon juice and all

SEVERAL SMALL PLATES OF A PARTICULAR DISH LOOK FAR MORE ATTRACTIVE, AND ARE EASIER TO SERVE FROM, THAN ONE BIG BOWL, SO KEEP AN EYE OUT FOR INTERESTING SERVING DISHES. THESE PIERCED-WARE PLATES SHOW THE LEMON AND MINT CABBAGE SALAD AND CARROT, DATE AND PECAN SALAD OFF TO PERFECTION.

the seasonings. Add the oil when they are fully combined. Pour the dressing over the cabbage and mix in the green peppers and courgettes, toss the salad thoroughly and chill. To serve, decorate with lemon quarters and mint sprigs.

HAM GLAZED WITH APRICOTS

This is a very useful recipe for any party. Most people like ham and this method of cooking makes it moist with a lovely flavour.

2 × 5 kg (10 lb) hams (it is easiest to buy them ready-cooked)	10 g (2 tsp) ground allspice
175 g (6 oz) demerara sugar	10 g (2 tsp) ground coriander
175 g (6 oz) apricot jam	300 ml (½ pint) apricot brandy or Amaretto liqueur
100 g (4 oz) wholegrain mustard	

APRICOTS AND ALMONDS IN AMARETTO

600 ml (1 pint) Amaretto liqueur	juice of 4 oranges
2 kg (4 lb) dried apricots	4.2 litres (7 pints) still cider
350 g (12 oz) demerara sugar	250 g (9 oz) whole blanched almonds

SERVES ABOUT 50

Heat the oven to 220°C (425°F), Gas Mark 7. Place one ham in a roasting tin. Peel off the skin with a knife and discard it if it has not already been removed. Using a small sharp knife, score diagonal lines across the whole area of fat and then in the opposite direction to make a diamond pattern. Take half the amount of apricot brandy or Amaretto and brush it across the skin liberally. Mix the sugar, apricot jam, mustard and spices together and divide the mixture in half. Spread one half well into the fat of the ham. I normally use my hand but you could use a spoon instead. If there is any of the measured half portion of liqueur left, sprinkle it over the spiced fat until it is all used up.

Bake the ham in the oven for 25-35 min-

utes or until the fat is crisp and golden brown. Then repeat the operation with the other ham and leave both hams to cool, well covered. Serve with Apricots and Almonds in Amaretto (see below).

Apricots and Almonds in Amaretto
Boil the cider, apricots, sugar and orange juice in a pan. Reduce the heat and simmer for approximately 15 minutes, or until the apricots are just soft. Strain out the apricots (keep to one side), and reboil the cider mixture until it thickens.

Fill clean, warm jam jars with the apricots, layering them carefully and adding the almonds at regular intervals. Pour in the Amaretto liqueur, dividing it equally between the jars. Top up the jars with the reboiled syrup and then cover each one with waxed paper. Seal when they have cooled. The jars can be stored in a refrigerator for several months.

SALMON IN CHAMPAGNE

Don't be discouraged and think you can't cope with a whole salmon. You can, and you'll find it a lot easier than you'd imagined. Choosing a suitable cooking dish is important. If you can't borrow a fish kettle from your fishmonger then use your largest roasting dish and fit the salmon into it, curving it if necessary. The finished dish looks very special and is usually a huge success.

4 × 2.5 kg (5 lb) whole salmon, gutted and cleaned	3 litres (5 pints) champagne
	8-9 cucumbers
3 litres (5 pints) fish stock	bunch of parsley

SERVES ABOUT 50

I have suggested using medium-sized salmon as they are easy to fit into a large roasting tin. If you have an enormous fish kettle then

32

BOTH THE HAM GLAZED
WITH APRICOTS AND THE
SALMON IN CHAMPAGNE,
WITH THEIR RESPECTIVE
ACCOMPANIMENTS, LOOK
VERY IMPRESSIVE BUT ARE
SURPRISINGLY EASY TO
MAKE. THE TRICK IS TO
ALLOW YOURSELF PLENTY
OF TIME AND, ABOVE ALL,
NOT TO PANIC!

of course you can just buy two or three gigantic fish. I always manage, however, by curving the fish slightly, using my largest roasting tin and cooking one fish at a time.

Wash the fish really well, inside and out. Mix about 900 ml (1½ pints) of fish stock with the same amount of champagne. Pour a little fish stock and champagne into the fish kettle or roasting tin and then carefully lay the fish inside the tin, bending it slightly if necessary. Cover with aluminium foil. Place in a pre-heated oven at 200°C (400°F), Gas Mark 6 for about 30 minutes. Then

take the fish out of the oven and test the middle to see if it is cooked. If it is, replace the foil and leave it to cool completely.

When the fish is cold, remove it from the pan (I use two fish slices to do this) and lay it on a board or work surface. Save the cooking juices for the mayonnaise recipe. Carefully peel off the skin and discard, then turn the fish over and repeat the operation on the other side. Lift the skinned fish carefully on to a large serving plate.

Now you must choose whether you want to serve it with or without the head. If you

any damage camouflaged by the decoration.

Using sharp kitchen scissors, snip the backbone away at the head and tail and lift it off. Please check really carefully, under a good light, that you have removed all the bones that you possibly can. It makes it much more pleasant for the guests not to have to keep extracting stray fish bones from each mouthful. Now replace the top fillet.

You can use aspic to decorate the fish, but I never do. Instead, I suggest using paper-thin slices of cucumber in an imitation of fish scales, with plenty of parsley and lemons. Slice the cucumber very thinly and cover the entire body with overlapping slices as shown in the picture. Place a tiny bunch of parsley inside the eye socket if you are keeping the head, and then spread some lemon quarters and parsley around the dish to finish. Serve with the Champagne Mayonnaise (see below). Repeat this operation for however many salmon you have cooked.

CHAMPAGNE MAYONNAISE

4 eggs (you can either use them whole or just use the yolks)	600 ml (1 pint) virgin olive oil
5 g (1 tsp) English mustard	salt and freshly ground black pepper
60 ml (4 tbsp) white wine vinegar	cooking liquid from the fish (see page 31–3)

MAKES 600 ML (1 PINT), SO MAKE 4 BATCHES

Put the eggs (I use whole eggs as I never seem to use up the whites for meringues), mustard and half the vinegar into the bowl of a food processor or blender. Process for 15-20 seconds.

Slowly add the oil with the machine still running, and continue to process until the mayonnaise is thick and creamy. Add the remaining vinegar. Then, depending on the thickness of the mayonnaise, stir in some cooking liquid from the fish until it is a

want to leave the head on, I would suggest that you remove the eye as this always seems to gaze reproachfully at the guests and doesn't make it look exactly appetizing! Cut off the fins and any small bones that are attached. Loosen the flesh around the head and then run an extremely sharp knife down the middle of the body. (If you use a blunt knife you will only tear the flesh.) Carefully lift off the top fillet with the fish slices or spatulas and place on one side. Don't get too worried about bits breaking off as the fishy jigsaw can be put back together again and

IT IS ALWAYS A GOOD IDEA TO OFFER A CHOICE OF DESSERTS: SOMETHING LIGHT AND FRUITY, SUCH AS THESE STRAWBERRIES IN COINTREAU, AND SOMETHING RATHER MORE SUBSTANTIAL, SUCH AS THIS CHOCOLATE PECAN PIE. DON'T BE SURPRISED IF MOST GUESTS CAST THEIR GOOD INTENTIONS TO THE WINDS AND HAVE A LITTLE OF EACH ONE!

creamy sauce of medium thickness. Add a little at a time or you will make the mayonnaise too runny.

STRAWBERRIES WITH COINTREAU

This recipe is quick and simple, yet utterly irresistible.

2 kg (4 lb) ripe strawberries	150-200 ml (5-7 fl oz) Cointreau

SERVES 10, SO MAKE 5 BATCHES

Wash the strawberries very briefly and remove the hulls. Chop any large strawberries into halves or quarters and pile them into a bowl. As you cover the base of the bowl add some Cointreau, then pour in the rest of the strawberries followed by the rest of the Cointreau. Gently toss the strawberries in the Cointreau and chill. If possible, keep gently turning the fruit in the liqueur during the next few hours. Do not make this dessert the day before it is needed because it will only keep well for a maximum of six hours. Serve with cream.

CHOCOLATE PECAN PIE

This recipe brings out the greedy side in most people. I have known my family to eat this with cream and ice cream and still be able to get up from the table! It really is delicious and seconds are nearly always requested.

PASTRY	
350 g (12 oz) self-raising flour	pinch of salt
225 g (8 oz) white vegetable fat	approx 100 ml (4 fl oz) cold water

FILLING	
175 g (6 oz) shelled pecan nuts	2 large eggs, beaten well
75 g (3 oz) butter	100 g (4 oz) self-raising flour
75 g (3 oz) demerara sugar	225 g (8 oz) good-quality plain chocolate
45 ml (3 tbsp) golden syrup	extra pecan nuts for decoration

SERVES 8-10, SO MAKE 5 BATCHES

Make the pastry by rubbing the fat into the sieved flour and salt until the mixture resembles breadcrumbs. Gradually add enough water to form a soft dough, but don't make it too wet. Roll out the pastry on a well-floured board and lift it into a greased 22.5-25 cm (9-10 in) flan or pie dish. Press well down and mark across the base with a fork. Cover with a sheet of greaseproof paper and fill with a layer of dry rice, peas or beans. Bake in a pre-heated oven at 190°C (375°F), Gas Mark 5 for 15 minutes. Remove the paper and rice or beans.

Cover the pastry base with pecan nuts. Put the butter in a pan and melt gently. Then remove from the heat and stir in the golden syrup, sugar and eggs. Sieve in the flour and stir again. Pour the mixture over the pecan nuts and bake in the oven at 170°C (325°F), Gas Mark 3 for about 30 minutes. While the pie is cooking, melt the chocolate in a bowl over some hot water. When the pie comes out of the oven, pour the melted chocolate over the top of the pie and decorate it with the extra pecan nuts. You can serve this pie hot or cold, but I usually serve it cold with some whipped cream mixed with a little maple syrup.

APRICOT, ORANGE AND AMARETTO WEDDING CAKE

I know that traditionally everyone has a fruit wedding cake but this is a lovely alternative. If, however, you are determined on a fruit cake base then use the recipe for the Christmas Cake (see pages 110–11). It has been used in our family for wedding cakes for many years and is well tried and tested.

CAKE	
900 g (2 lb) butter	900 g (2 lb) semolina
70 g (14 tsp) grated orange rind	900 g (2 lb) ground almonds
900 g (2 lb) castor sugar	400 ml (14 fl oz) unsweetened orange juice
14 eggs	
35 g (7 tsp) baking powder	

AMARETTO SYRUP	
900 ml (1½ pint) Amaretto liqueur	900 ml (1½ pint) unsweetened orange juice
	900 g (2 lb) castor sugar

AMARETTO GLAZE	
450 g (1 lb) apricot jam	90 ml (6 tbsp) Amaretto liqueur

ORANGE BUTTERCREAM ICING	
700 g (24 oz) butter	apricot cake colouring (yellow is not such a good finished colour)
1.3 kg (3 lb) icing sugar	
90 ml (6 tbsp) orange juice, strained	

This is a more modern cake with a soft natural decoration that you can easily manage. I much prefer a soft effect like this to stiff, formal piping and ornamentation. If you're nervous and want to practice, then why not try a scaled-down version for a family weekend?

You will need three deep cake tins, sizes 15 cm (6 in), 22.5 cm (9 in) and 30 cm (12 in). These should be well-greased with butter and the bases should all be lined with circles of buttered greaseproof paper. You should also buy, or make, three cardboard rounds in the same sizes as the tins, which look like very thin cakeboards. These will go between the layers of cake.

First make the syrup (this can be done up to a couple of days in advance). Mix the orange juice and sugar in a saucepan, stirring constantly until the sugar has dissolved. Bring to the boil and simmer uncovered for at least 5 or 6 minutes. Add the Amaretto liqueur and simmer again for another couple of minutes. Remove from the heat, leave to cool and then store in the fridge.

Cream the butter, orange rind and sugar in a mixing bowl, using an electric beater, until they are light and fluffy. One by one, beat in the eggs until well combined. Make sure the bowl is large enough to take all the remaining ingredients – if not, transfer the mixture to a larger mixing bowl.

Stir in the semolina and half the orange juice, then add the ground almonds, baking powder and the rest of the orange juice. Divide the mixture between the cake tins; try to ensure they all come up to the same height or you will end up with cakes of uneven depth. Bake in a pre-heated oven, at 170°C (325°F), Gas Mark 3 for between 30 and 50 minutes, depending on the size of the cake tin. The cake is cooked when it feels firm when tapped and can be pulled away slightly from the sides of the tin.

Once a layer is out of the oven, make a few small holes with a wooden satay stick or cocktail stick all over the top of the cake (do not remove it from the tin yet) and gently pour some of the syrup over the cake. Return it to the oven for about 4 or 5 minutes, then remove from the oven and turn the cake out on a wire rack. Make more holes in the base this time, add more syrup and leave the cake to cool.

Amaretto Glaze
Mix the apricot jam and Amaretto liqueur in a small saucepan and heat gently until it becomes liquid enough to be spread with a brush. Brush all three cake layers all over with the glaze.

Take the three cardboard layers, and placing each cake layer on its matching piece of cardboard, place the 30 cm (12 in) cake on the bottom, the 22.5 cm (9 in) cake on top of it and the 18 cm (6 in) cake on top of that.

Orange Buttercream Icing
Beat the butter and icing sugar together in a bowl with an electric mixer until the mixture is light and fluffy. Add the orange juice a little at a time until you have a consistency that will spread well but keep its shape. Finally, beat in a tiny amount of apricot food colouring to slightly tint the mixture. No bright orange bowls of icing, please!

Spread the buttercream icing all over the three layers of cake, swirling it as you go to give a slightly textured finish. You may also pipe on some swirls or rosettes if you wish. Then, having previously chosen your flowers, stick them into the cake. I always wrap the ends of the stalks in a little clingfilm to prevent any sap leaching into the icing. Cut the stalks very short. Although I am suggesting that you use the cake like a block of floral foam, this does not mean criss-crossing it with flower stems. Choose dainty flowers and leaves and just use enough for effect – too many and it will look like a heap of flowers. You can decorate the cake with the buttercream the day before but don't add the flowers until the last convenient moment.

FACING PAGE: THE CENTREPIECE OF ANY WEDDING IS THE CAKE, BUT IT DOESN'T HAVE TO BE THE USUAL FRUIT CAKE COVERED IN ROYAL ICING. IN FACT, IT CAN BE VERY TIME-CONSUMING AND DIFFICULT TO ACHIEVE A PROFESSIONAL FINISH WITH ROYAL ICING, WHICH IS WHY I ENJOY USING BUTTERCREAM SO MUCH BECAUSE IT LOOKS BEST WITH A SLIGHTLY TEXTURED FINISH.

SUMMER TEA PARTIES

Entertaining at tea-time has become less popular over the years, which I find sad. The tradition of having people over for tea is convenient, because cakes, pastries or scones can be made well in advance and are inexpensive when compared with the cost of giving a dinner party. I think traditional teas are also very enjoyable. Winter tea-time parties can be enjoyed around a blazing log fire with crumpets and muffins, home-made jam and cakes. Summer tea parties may well mean different surroundings but they have special benefits that winter teas do not.

Awarm summery afternoon in an English garden is one of my happy memories from childhood, eating lemon curd and scones, biscuits and cakes. Tea can be a close family occasion or a gathering of friends and neighbours, and is much more relaxed than a formal evening event. If young children are involved then they can race around the garden without the constrictions of polite grown-up behaviour.

One of the best parties we've ever been to had a Twenties theme, and everyone wore flapper costumes or striped blazers and boaters. There were punts on the river and hampers full of traditional English tea-time food on the banks of the river. Why not entertain your friends during an afternoon for a change? Perhaps we should all try to revive the tradition of the English tea.

THIS SIMPLE JUG OF ANEMONES AND HOLLY LEAVES HAS TREMENDOUS IMPACT, AND TAKES ONLY MINUTES TO ARRANGE.

TOMATO AND MINT SANDWICHES WITH ORANGE CHEESE

Sandwiches are much maligned but they are actually a very practical way of presenting food. This combination raises the level of sandwiches from practical to perfection; they are indescribably delicious.

16 slices bread, preferably thick-cut granary	12 mint leaves or sprigs
	8 medium tomatoes
150 g (6 oz) curd cheese	salt and black pepper
zest and juice of 1 orange	
SERVES 8	

Mix the juice and zest of the orange with the curd cheese. Spread all 16 slices of bread thinly with the orange cheese mixture. Process or very finely chop all the mint leaves and sprinkle them equally over 8 slices of bread. Slice the tomatoes thinly and place the slices on top of the mint – 1 tomato per slice of bread. Then grind some

black pepper and sprinkle some sea salt over the tomatoes, and place the second piece of bread over the top. Don't cut the crusts off, they're good for you! Cut in halves or quarters and wrap in clingfilm if you are preparing them in advance.

CHICKEN AND BACON SANDWICHES WITH AVOCADO MAYONNAISE

Here is another wonderful sandwich filling. These sandwiches are also ideal for packed lunches.

16 slices bread, preferably thick-cut granary	8 rashers of well-cooked back bacon
	4 cooked chicken breast fillets
1 large avocado	a little fresh dill
100 g (4 oz) home-made or bought mayonnaise	salt and black pepper
SERVES 8	

Halve the avocado and prise out the stone. Scoop all the flesh out of the avocado, including as much of the brightest green flesh, very close to the skin, as possible. Put into a basin and mix in the mayonnaise. Add salt and pepper to taste. Spread this mixture equally over the 16 slices of bread.

Using scissors, chop the bacon into small pieces and slice the chicken breasts thinly. Take a slice of bread, scatter some chopped bacon over it and then place the equivalent of half a chicken breast on top. Sprinkle a little fresh dill over the chicken and cover with another slice of bread. Cut into squares or triangles. Wrap the sandwiches in clingfilm and store in the fridge if you will be making them in advance.

RHUBARB AND CHAMPAGNE JAM

I think this is a lovely combination of ingredients, and it is one of the jams we make for sale in our shop. You could cheat and use white wine instead of champagne to reduce the cost if you wished.

675 g (1½ lb) rhubarb	675 g (1½ lb) sugar
2 large apples	40 ml (1½ fl oz) lemon juice
300 ml (½ pint) champagne	

MAKES ABOUT 900 G (2 LB)

Peel, core and chop the apples. Chop the rhubarb and put the apples and rhubarb, with the champagne, into a large pan. Cover the pan and bring to the boil, then simmer gently for 15 minutes until the fruit is soft. Add the sugar and lemon juice. Make sure there is plenty of room in the pan for the jam to boil rapidly at a later stage.

Cook the mixture gently, stirring constantly, until all the sugar has dissolved. Then bring to the boil and boil very rapidly, uncovered, for about 40 minutes. (If you are using a thermometer, setting point is at 221°F [105°C]. If not, spoon a little jam on to a chilled saucer, allow to cool and then push your finger across its surface – it will wrinkle when it has reached setting point.) Have ready some warm clean jam jars and fill them with the jam. Cover each jar with a waxed paper disc. When cool, seal the jars and label them clearly.

IN THE RUSH OF MODERN LIVING, JAM-MAKING SEEMS TO BE A DYING ART, SO WHY NOT STAGE YOUR OWN REVIVAL WITH THIS RHUBARB AND CHAMPAGNE JAM?

STRAWBERRY AND ORANGE JAM

The orange helps to bring out the flavour of the strawberries – and who can resist strawberry jam?

1 kg (2¼ lb) ripe strawberries	675 g (1½ lb) sugar with pectin
1 large juicy orange	45 ml (3 tbsp) Cointreau
150 ml (¼ pint) water	

————— MAKES ABOUT 900 G (2 LB) —————

If the strawberries are very dirty you should wash them briefly, but they retain more flavour if you just wipe them carefully with a damp cloth. Hull the strawberries and halve any that are particularly large. Place in a bowl with the grated zest of the orange, then squeeze the orange and add the juice. Leave to soak for at least 30 minutes, but preferably longer.

Boil the sugar and water for about 5 minutes and then add the strawberry mixture. Boil rapidly until setting point is reached. (If you are using a thermometer, setting point is at 221°F [105°C]. If not, spoon a little jam on to a chilled saucer, allow to cool and then push your finger across its surface – it will wrinkle when it has reached setting point.) Remove from the heat and stir in the Cointreau. Pour into warmed, clean jam jars, cover and seal. Label the jars clearly.

DEVONSHIRE FRUIT SCONES

Here is a scone recipe with a difference. The scones are so simple to make that my nephew even baked some at school – they were a great success.

225 g (8 oz) self-raising flour	50 g (2 oz) butter
pinch of salt	50 g (2 oz) sugar
pinch of cinnamon	1 small cooking apple
5 g (1 level tsp) baking powder	1 small pear
	85 ml (3½ fl oz) milk plus a little extra

————— MAKES ABOUT 12 —————

ANYONE WITH THE WILLPOWER TO RESIST A CREAM TEA LIKE THIS DESERVES A MEDAL; I AM NOT ONE OF THEM!

Pre-heat the oven to 200°C (400°F), Gas Mark 6. Place a baking sheet in the oven to heat up. Sift together the flour, salt, baking powder and cinnamon. Rub the butter into the flour until it looks like breadcrumbs. Stir in the sugar. Peel, core and very finely chop the apple and pear and add the fruit to the mixture. Add the milk and mix until you have a soft dough.

Place the dough on a very well-floured board or worktop, roll out to about 12 mm (½ in) thick and cut into small rounds. Place them on the pre-heated baking sheet, brush with milk and sprinkle with sugar. Bake for about 15 minutes until golden brown. Serve split and filled with Devonshire clotted cream and Rhubarb and Champagne Jam (see page 41).

SUMMER FRUIT CAKE

This cake makes a refreshing change from the ordinary fruit cake made with dried fruit. It stays very moist and the fruit you use can be varied widely according to what is in season or what you have to hand.

1050 g (2¼ lb) fresh fruit (such as apples, plums, greengages, peaches, pineapples, bananas or dates)	300 g (11 oz) sugar
	5 medium eggs
	275 g (10 oz) plain flour
	2 g (½ tsp) salt
225 g (8 oz) unsalted butter	

——— MAKES A 22.5 CM (9 IN) CAKE ———

Keep 2 apples, or your chosen fruit, for decoration. Wash, peel and core the remaining fruit and cut into fairly large pieces. Cream together the butter and sugar, then add the eggs one at a time, beating the mixture well between each addition.

Sift together the flour and salt and fold into the mixture. Stir in the fruit, then turn the mixture into a greased and floured 22.5 cm (9 in) square cake tin. Peel and core the reserved fruit and cut into circles. Arrange

on the top of the mixture, pressing them lightly into the mixture.

Bake in a pre-heated oven at 170°C (325°F), Gas Mark 3, for 1½ to 2 hours until the cake is firm to the touch. Cool for a few minutes before turning out on to a wire rack.

THIS VASE OF MIXED ROSES CAPTURES THE ESSENCE OF SUMMER FOR ME. IT WOULD MAKE A LOVELY DECORATION FOR YOUR TEA TABLE, EVEN IF IT WERE LAID OUT IN THE GARDEN.

SQUIRREL CAKE

This is a recipe of my mother's, and although there are no nuts in the mixture it nevertheless tastes very nutty and delicious. It is also very economical to make.

100 g (4 oz) margarine	2 large eggs, beaten
100 g (4 oz) sugar	15 ml (1 tbsp) cold water
100 g (4 oz) self-raising flour	10 g (2 tsp) instant coffee granules
MAKES A 17.5 CM (7 IN) CAKE	
SQUIRREL'S CREAM	
425 ml (¾ pint) double cream	45 g (3 tbsp) chopped hazelnuts, plus extra for decoration
45 ml (3 tbsp) Tia Maria liqueur	

Grease and line two 17.5 cm (7 in) sponge tins. Cream together the margarine and sugar until white and creamy. Add the beaten eggs a little at a time and beat well (no cheating with an electric mixer – the results are much better by hand). Using a metal spoon fold in the sifted flour and add the cold water until a soft consistency is reached. At the very last moment fold in instant coffee granules.

Spoon the mixture into the two sandwich tins and spread evenly with a palette knife. Bake in a pre-heated oven at 190°C (375°F), Gas Mark 5 for about 20 minutes. Remove from the oven when they are cooked and turn out on to a wire rack to cool. When cold, sandwich the two cakes together with the Squirrel's Cream (see below).

Squirrel's Cream
Whip the cream and add a little sugar if you wish. Fold in the Tia Maria and the hazelnuts. Use as a filling and decoration on the top of the cake. Sprinkle the top of the cake with the extra hazelnuts.

HERE IS THE SQUIRREL CAKE ON THE STAND, AND A RICH FRUIT CAKE, MADE FROM THE CHRISTMAS CAKE (see pages 110–11).

LEMON AND MINT COOLER

Old-fashioned lemonade is delicious, and much better for you than the commercially available varieties, so do try some. It's very refreshing on a hot summer's day.

2½ litres (4¼ pints) water	large handful of mint leaves
juice of 8 lemons	extra mint leaves for garnishing
75 g (3 oz) castor sugar	

— **SERVES ABOUT 8** —

Chop the mint leaves coarsely and place in a large bowl with the sugar. Pound the two ingredients together well so that the sugar takes up the flavour of the mint leaves. Heat the water to boiling point and pour over the mint and sugar. Add the lemon juice and leave to cool.

When the mixture has cooled, carefully strain it through a fine sieve and chill in the fridge. Serve in the prettiest glasses you can find, garnished with ice, slivers of lemon and sprigs of mint.

THIS LEMON AND MINT COOLER IS THE PERFECT DRINK FOR A SUMMER'S AFTERNOON.

HARVEST AND THANKSGIVING

Whether you are celebrating harvest-time or giving a traditional American Thanksgiving dinner, the autumn is a great time of year for entertaining. There are several occasions that can provide you with an excuse for throwing a party, whether it be Hallowe'en, Bonfire Night or autumn generally. The leaves are turning incredibly beautiful shades of red and gold and the weather is sometimes wonderfully crisp, sunny and invigorating. Brisk autumn walks through crunchy leaves always help to develop an appetite, especially if there's a nip in the air and you're hurrying home to a log fire and a large tea!

Those of you who are still basking in warm sunshine at this time of year probably don't envy the rest of us our changeable climate but it is still a good time of year to celebrate.

TOMATO, ORANGE AND CHERVIL SOUP

One of my favourite soups, this tastes really delicate and the orange is a delicious companion to the tomato. My daughter said it tasted nothing like her favourite canned tomato soup – she meant it as a complaint but I took it as a marvellous compliment!

2.3 kg (5 lb) fresh tomatoes	75 g (3 oz) butter
75 g (3 oz) tomato purée	75 g (3 oz) flour
4 large juicy oranges	1 small garlic clove
900 ml (1½ pints) rich vegetable or chicken stock	10 g (2 tsp) brown sugar
	small handful of fresh chervil
2 medium onions	salt and black pepper
2 large carrots	

SERVES 6-8

Fill a saucepan three-quarters full of water and bring to the boil. Make a cross in the skin of each tomato and one by one dip them into the boiling water. Leave each tomato in the water for a few seconds until the skin starts to peel back. Remove from the water and, as soon as you can touch the tomato, peel off the skin. Once all the tomatoes are peeled, chop them into quarters and remove and discard the cores and pips.

Chop the carrots and onions and gently fry them in butter until the onion is transparent but not brown. Add the flour and mix well, then cook for about 10 minutes. Add the tomato purée, stock and the zest and juice of the oranges and cook until a thick, smooth consistency is achieved. Add the chopped tomatoes, garlic and sugar, and season to taste. Simmer for 30 minutes.

Liquidize the soup and pass it through a fine sieve. Reserve some pieces of chervil to decorate the soup and then finely chop the remainder. Warm the soup through before serving and at the last minute stir in the finely chopped chervil. Garnish each bowl with a sprig of chervil and hand round some *croûtons* to accompany the soup.

This soup can be made the day before and kept in the refrigerator until needed. It's time-consuming to use fresh tomatoes but the flavour is well worth the effort. Tinned tomatoes taste very third-rate in comparison for this recipe.

IF SERVED IN LARGE BOWLS WITH SOME FRESH CRUSTY BREAD, THIS TOMATO, ORANGE AND CHERVIL SOUP WOULD MAKE A DELICIOUS LUNCH DISH.

TURKEY IN ROWANBERRY SAUCE

Turkey fillets are quick and easy to cook, but they don't have quite the ceremonial pomp of an entire bird carved at the table. As far as I'm concerned, the relief of not having to worry about cooking a huge turkey and serving up the disguised leftovers for days and days more than compensates for any lack of looks.

8 turkey escalopes or breast fillets	50 g (2 oz) unsalted butter
600 ml (1 pint) rich chicken or turkey stock	50 g (2 oz) flour
	300 ml (½ pint) medium white wine
175 g (6 oz) rowanberry jelly (see below)	75 ml (3 fl oz) sunflower oil
SERVES 8	
ROWANBERRY JELLY	
2 kg (4½ lb) rowanberries	sugar as needed
45 ml (3 tbsp) lemon juice	
MAKES 2.3 KG (5 LB)	

Melt the butter in a pan and add the flour. Cook gently, stirring constantly, for about 10 minutes. Add the stock slowly, whisking with a metal balloon whisk until the stock is incorporated and there are no lumps. Add the jelly in teaspoonfuls so it is distributed around the pan, and cook gently, stirring occasionally, until the jelly has dissolved. If the mixture is too thick you can thin it down with the wine, or you can use water if you prefer. The sauce can be made in advance and then reheated when needed.

Using a large frying pan, pour in the oil and cook four of the escalopes at once (depending on their size and that of the pan). Cook until the escalopes are gently brown on both sides and there is no sign of pink in the middle. Keep them warm in a hot oven until you have cooked the others. Reheat the sauce, arrange the escalopes on a hot serving dish, pour on the sauce and garnish with something green; parsley, watercress or basil, perhaps.

Rowanberry Jelly

Strip all the rowanberries off their stalks (they should be weighed without their stalks) and place in a pan with enough water to cover them. Cook them gently until they are just soft – usually about 15 minutes. Then add the lemon juice and strain through a jelly bag or piece of muslin overnight. I usually turn a stool upside down and use that as a rest for the jelly bag.

The following day, measure the resulting juice and pour it into a pan. For every 600 ml (1 pint) of juice add 400 g (14 oz) sugar. Stir over a gentle heat while the sugar dissolves, then boil rapidly until setting point is reached. (If you are using a thermometer, setting point is at 221°F [105°C]. If not, spoon a little jelly on to a chilled saucer, allow to cool and then push your finger across its surface – it will wrinkle when it has reached setting point.)

Have some warm clean jars ready and, once the mixture has cooled down slightly, pour it into the jars, cover each one with a waxed paper circle and seal tightly.

BROCCOLI WITH ALMONDS

Broccoli is not only extremely good for you, it is delicious as well. It is very important not to overcook the broccoli.

1-2 large heads broccoli (approximately 1 kg [2 lb])	50 g (2 oz) flaked almonds
	25 g (1 oz) unsalted butter
SERVES 8	

Cut the broccoli into florets and wash thoroughly, then boil or steam the broccoli until just tender. Serve sprinkled with flaked almonds and dotted with the butter.

PUMPKIN STUFFED WITH SPICED RICE AND NUTS

This makes a good centrepiece for your feast. It doesn't take long to scoop out the flesh, and it's not wasted because you can make a pumpkin soup or pumpkin pie with it.

225 g (8 oz) white rice	45 ml (3 tbsp) unsweetened orange juice
100 g (4 oz) pecan nuts	
100 g (4 oz) pistachio nuts	5 g (1 tsp) ground allspice
100 g (4 oz) dried apricots	salt and pepper
	1 large pumpkin

SERVES AT LEAST 8

Chop the apricots roughly (I use scissors) and put in a small bowl with the orange juice. Cook the rice for 15-20 minutes according to the manufacturer's instructions and then drain well. Mix in the pecans, pistachios, apricots and juice, then add the allspice, salt and pepper and stir well. Taste and add more seasonings if you want.

Serve by hollowing out a pumpkin and filling it with the rice mixture. The rice could be cooked in advance but do not incorporate any of the other ingredients until an hour or so before they are needed, then reheat it all before serving.

COURGETTES WITH SESAME

The sesame oil imparts a subtle flavour that is different and delicious.

8 medium-sized courgettes	25 g (1 oz) unsalted butter
30 ml (2 tbsp) sesame oil	15 g (1 tbsp) sesame seeds

SERVES 8

Top and tail the courgettes and then cut them in half lengthwise. Cut each half down the middle and then into quarters, to give chunky sticks of courgette. Heat the sesame oil and butter in a shallow frying pan and toss in the courgette sticks. Cook for about 5-7 minutes or until they are just done (do not let them turn brown), and serve sprinkled with the sesame seeds.

PEAR AND BRAMBLE PIE

This is a very popular pie with everyone who attends my courses. Avoid using frozen pears because they may make the filling too watery.

675 g (1½ lb) self-raising flour	450 g (1 lb) blackberries (fresh or frozen)
450 g (1 lb) white vegetable fat	45 g (3 tbsp) demerara sugar
6-8 Conference pears	water

SERVES 8-10

Peel, core and slice the pears. Cook them gently in enough water to cover with 30 g (2 tbsp) of the sugar – it is important to cook them gently to keep their shape. Leave them to cool. Cook the blackberries with a little water and the remaining 15 g (1 tbsp) of sugar and then leave to cool. It is better to keep the pears and blackberries separate – it makes no difference to the taste but does improve the finished look of the filling.

Make the pastry by rubbing the fat into

IF YOU HAVE SUCH A GLUT OF BLACKBERRIES THAT YOU CAN EASILY SPARE SOME, A FEW BERRY-LADEN SPRAYS MAKE A STUNNING ARRANGEMENT.

the flour until it resembles breadcrumbs, then add about a cupful of water to form a soft dough. Divide the dough in half and gently roll out the first half on a very well-floured board. Lift the pastry by folding it over the rolling pin and line a greased 30 cm (12 in) dish with it. The pie is easiest to serve if the dish has straight sides. Mould the pastry round the edges of the dish and trim off any excess.

Drain the pears and blackberries (save some of the juice), still keeping them separate. Cover the base of the pie with the pear slices and then cover them with the blackberries. Spoon a little of the juice over the fruit and discard the rest. Roll out the other half of the pastry and, having moistened the edges of the bottom layer of pastry with water, place the pastry over the pie to make a lid. Press gently around the edges and trim off any excess. Brush the top of

WE HAVE A PEAR AND AN APPLE TREE IN OUR GARDEN, PLUS BLACKBERRIES THAT RAMBLE OVER THE BACK FENCE. WE THEREFORE TRY ALL THE POSSIBLE COMBINATIONS IN PIES, AND I ACTUALLY PREFER PEAR AND BLACKBERRY TO THE MORE USUAL APPLE AND BLACKBERRY MIXTURE.

the pie with milk, or a mixture of milk and egg yolk, then use any scraps of pastry to decorate the top of the pie with leaves, apples or any other design you like. Bake in a pre-heated oven at 200°C (400°F), Gas Mark 6 for 25-30 minutes or until the pastry is cooked and golden brown.

ICED CHOCOLATE AND AMARETTO PUDDINGS

This must be served straight from the freezer as it melts quite quickly and is nicest when thoroughly frozen. I use fairly large ramekins, but if you wanted to use smaller dishes you could cut down on the ingredients or keep to these quantities and make more puddings.

50 g (2 oz) unsalted butter	175 g (6 oz) granulated sugar
300 g (11 oz) good-quality dark chocolate	100 g (4 oz) blanched almonds
5 medium eggs	water
100 g (4 oz) castor sugar	whipped cream for decoration
30 mg (2 tbsp) Amaretto liqueur	
175 ml (6 fl oz) double cream	chocolate curls or leaves for decoration

SERVES 8

To make the almond praline, mix the granulated sugar and 30 ml (2 tbsp) of water in a heavy-bottomed pan. Stir constantly without boiling until the sugar has dissolved. Chop the almonds finely, then increase the heat and boil the water and sugar without stirring until the mixture is a pale golden brown. Stir in the almonds and pour on to a baking tray lined with buttered greaseproof paper. Leave to set. Once the praline has set, chop it into small pieces and store in an airtight container.

Melt the chocolate in a heat-proof bowl over a pan of boiling water. Melt the butter in a separate saucepan, then combine it with the chocolate, off the heat. Beat the eggs and castor sugar (preferably using an electric mixer) until they are thick and creamy, then fold in the chocolate mixture. Whip the double cream and then add it, the praline and Amaretto to the mixture. Pour into individual ramekin dishes or small bowls and freeze. To serve, decorate with a rosette of whipped cream and a chocolate curl or leaf.

I CLASS THESE ICED CHOCOLATE AND AMARETTO PUDDINGS UNDER THE HEADING OF 'IRRESISTIBLE': SOMEHOW GUESTS CAN ALWAYS FIND ROOM FOR THEM!

DINNER PARTIES

I think having a dinner party is one of the happiest ways of entertaining. As well as the pleasure of talking with friends, you can also share recipes and new ideas. If you are pushed for time, why not ask the other guests to bring the puddings or starters? Most people think it's a great idea and it certainly lifts the burden of cooking an entire meal.

Some people seem to worry desperately about producing a meal for friends. It's understandable to worry if you are entertaining strangers or someone you want to impress, but having friends to dinner should be enjoyable for all of you. If they are going to be hypercritical of your food then perhaps it's time to pick a new bunch of friends! The point of a dinner party with friends is to have a good time and catch up on the news, not to spend all the evening in the kitchen, finally emerging with a wild-eyed look of despair and feeling (and looking) as though you have spent the last two hours in a sauna.

f you are really worried about cooking for more than your usual number, it is a good idea to cut out any starters and serve fresh fruit (buy the nicest you can find) and cheese and biscuits to follow the main course. That way you only have to produce a limited amount of dishes and will have less to feel anxious about. Many of these dishes, however, are fairly simple and, having road-tested them all, I can assure you they go down well with everyone.

FIGS IN PASTRY NESTS

Being a vegetarian need not mean having a slice of Cheddar cheese instead of a main course or living only on omelettes. These fig nests are delicious and can be served with the chicken for non-veggies or in place of it for vegetarians. Although my husband is never likely to be totally weaned away from meat, he certainly enjoyed this alternative and would recommend it to other meat-eating types.

8 bought or home-made vol-au-vent cases	225 g (8 oz) small mushrooms
12-14 dried figs	3-4 spring onions
75 ml (5 tbsp) tawny port	50 g (2 oz) butter
	25 g (1 oz) flour
	30 ml (2 tbsp) water

SERVES 8

Soak the figs in the port for as long as is convenient, but preferably 2-3 hours. Chop the spring onions. Melt the butter in a pan and gently sauté the spring onions until partly cooked. Sprinkle the flour into the pan and stir well, then cook for five minutes. Do not let the mixture become too dark brown; it should be a golden colour.

Chop the mushrooms and drain the figs. Chop the figs and add to the onion mixture. Add the mushrooms, tawny port and water, then simmer gently until the figs are soft and the whole mixture is fairly thick. Spoon into the vol-au-vent cases and warm through in a pre-heated oven, at 170°C (325°F), Gas Mark 3. If any fig mixture is left over, you can keep it warm until the vol-au-vents are ready to serve, then pile on more fig mixture so that it pours out of the cases in a decorative manner.

HOT BRIE WITH HAZELNUTS ON A WATERCRESS SAUCE

This is one of my favourite recipes in the book. As you can guess, we are very keen on Brie, but you can make this dish with another cheese if you prefer. You could also make smaller portions of a variety of cheeses, and serve your guests with a selection.

350 g (12 oz) ground hazelnuts	675-900 g (1½-2 lb) small whole Brie
225 g (8 oz) granary breadcrumbs	50 g (2 oz) self-raising flour
	4 large eggs, beaten

WATERCRESS SAUCE

1 bunch fresh watercress	100 g (4 oz) plain Greek yoghurt
1 handful of fresh parsley	30 ml (2 tbsp) mayonnaise
30 g (2 tbsp) fresh chives	22 ml (1½ tbsp) lemon juice
15 g (1 tbsp) fresh dill	salt and black pepper
	sprigs of watercress for decoration

SERVES 8

Mix the hazelnuts and the breadcrumbs together. Cut the Brie into eight equal pieces. Coat each piece with flour then brush on the egg, or dip the cheese in the egg, and roll in the crumb mixture. Dip the cheese in the egg a second time, and roll it in the nuts and breadcrumbs again. Cover a baking sheet with a piece of greaseproof paper and place the pieces of cheese on it until they are needed.

Deep-fry the pieces of cheese for about 1-2 minutes and then place in the oven,

MANY MEAT-EATERS
BELIEVE THAT
VEGETARIAN FOOD IS A
BYWORD FOR DREARY
AND WORTHY
CONCOCTIONS THAT BEAR
A CLOSE RESEMBLANCE TO
SHREDDED CARDBOARD:
THESE TWO DISHES – HOT
BRIE WITH HAZELNUTS ON
A WATERCRESS SAUCE AND
FIGS IN PASTRY NESTS –
SHOULD GIVE THEM
PLENTY OF FOOD FOR
THOUGHT!

pre-heated to 180°C (350°F), Gas Mark 4, for another 4-5 minutes. Do not leave the Brie in the fat or the oven for too long, because the cheese will run everywhere and look terrible. Serve on a pool of chilled watercress sauce (see below) with Bath Oliver or water biscuits.

Note: You could just as easily use Camembert instead of Brie, and the triangular portions are ideal for this recipe.

Watercress Sauce
Place all the ingredients in the bowl of a food processor and process for 20-30 seconds until well incorporated. If you do not have a food processor or blender you should mince all the herbs, or chop them very finely, and mix well with the other ingredients.

To serve, spoon a puddle of sauce on to the middle of the plate, place a hot Brie portion on top, and decorate with a sprig of watercress.

CHICKEN IN APPLE AND PEAR CIDER

Chicken is usually a very safe choice for a dinner party. I try hard, particularly when I'm entertaining people attending my courses, to choose the safest combination of foods and tastes that I can find, while still cooking something delicious.

2 medium-sized chickens	5 g (1 tsp) ground ginger
300 ml (½ pint) apple cider	5 g (1 tsp) ground allspice
300 ml (½ pint) pear cider	5 g (1 tsp) ground cinnamon
100 g (4 oz) self-raising flour	salt and black pepper to taste
50 g (2 oz) dark brown sugar	pears and apples for decoration

SERVES 8

Thoroughly wash and clean the chickens. Mix together the apple and pear cider and

FACING PAGE: I NEVER COOK ANYTHING TOO ADVENTUROUS FOR PEOPLE I DON'T KNOW VERY WELL, BECAUSE NOTHING IS MORE EMBARRASSING FOR A GUEST THAN BEING SERVED WITH FOOD HE OR SHE REALLY CANNOT FACE EATING. HERE, CHICKEN IN APPLE AND PEAR CIDER IS ACCOMPANIED BY BRUSSELS SPROUTS WITH MULTI-COLOURED PEPPERS AND CARROTS AND PINK PEPPERCORNS FOR A VERY COLOURFUL MAIN COURSE.

leave the two chickens in the cider for about 24 hours before you want to cook them. Keep turning the chickens so that all sides are soaked in the marinade.

Remove the chickens from the marinade. In a large mixing bowl, combine the flour, spices, salt and pepper. Roll the chickens in this mixture until they are well coated. Place in an ovenproof dish and bake in a pre-heated oven at 190°C (375°F), Gas Mark 5 for 30-45 minutes. While the chickens are cooking, mix together the remaining marinade and the sugar. Remove the chickens from the oven and pour over the marinade and sugar mixture. Bake the chickens for a further 20-30 minutes until the juices run clear when you stick a skewer into the legs.

Remove the chickens from the oven and cut into quarters. Serve with some juice and slices of apple and pear that have been warmed through rather than cooked.

BRUSSELS SPROUTS WITH MULTI-COLOURED PEPPERS

Most of my family hate Brussels sprouts, so the only time I can cook them is when we have guests. This makes a lovely colourful dish but don't overcook the sprouts or you'll ruin them.

1 kg (2 lb) Brussels sprouts	1 green pepper
	1 yellow pepper
1 red pepper	salt and black pepper

SERVES 8

Slice the base from each sprout and peel off the outer leaves. Score a cross into each stem to help the cooking process. Halve the peppers, remove the seeds and then chop into small to medium squares. Either boil or steam the Brussels sprouts until just tender, adding the peppers for the last 5 minutes of cooking. Drain well and serve immediately.

CARROTS AND PINK PEPPERCORNS

Carrots are a fairly safe choice of vegetable because most people like them. The secret, though, is to make sure you don't overcook them; soft squidgy carrots are horrible and remind me of my school meals many, many years ago.

900 g (2 lb) carrots	25 g (1 oz) butter
30 g (2 tbsp) pink peppercorns	

SERVES 8

Top and tail the carrots and peel them thinly. Chop them in half lengthwise and then into thick julienne strips. Boil or steam for a short time until they are just tender. To serve, place in a suitable dish, then sprinkle the pink peppercorns over the carrots and dot with the butter.

MANGO HEAVEN

Much as we all enjoy puddings, it can be hard to find room after two previous courses for anything very filling. It's better to save dishes like home-made apple pie for a two-course meal when everyone will have room to do it justice. This pudding was invented when I was given a box of lovely ripe mangoes and, having made some mango chutney and every other mango recipe I could think of, still had some fruit left. It's easy, very quick and usually very popular.

2 ripe mangoes	300 ml (½ pint) plain Greek yoghurt
300 ml (½ pint) extra thick double cream	100 g (4 oz) flaked almonds, toasted

SERVES 8

Peel the mangoes and remove as much flesh as possible from the large stones. Discard the stones. Combine the mangoes, yoghurt

ONE OF THE JOYS OF HAVING A GARDEN IS BEING ABLE TO GROW COLOURFUL ANNUALS AND PERENNIALS THAT GO ON FLOWERING ALL SUMMER LONG WITH LITTLE OR NO ATTENTION FROM ME. THEY MAKE WONDERFUL FLOWERS FOR INFORMAL ARRANGEMENTS AND OFTEN LOOK BEST WHEN CRAMMED HIGGLEDY-PIGGLEDY INTO JUGS OR VASES.

ABOVE: DIETERS BEWARE!
MANGO HEAVEN MAY BE
LOADED WITH CALORIES
BUT IT'S ALSO QUITE
DELICIOUS.

FACING PAGE: TWO
TREATS THAT SHOULD
ENSURE THE SUCCESS OF
ANY DINNER PARTY:
CHOCOLATE DIPPED
FRUITS AND DEVON CREAM
TRUFFLES WITH
ELDERBERRY WINE.

and cream in a food processor and process for about 20-30 seconds. You can also make this dessert in a blender or by hand, using an electric or manual whisk.

Choose some pretty, individual glass or ceramic containers and fill with layers of the mango mixture and flaked almonds. Sprinkle more flaked almonds on the top. Chill in the fridge for at least 2-3 hours before serving.

CHOCOLATE DIPPED FRUITS

I defy any normal person (unless they loathe or are allergic to chocolate) to be able to resist these. The main trouble I have is stopping small hands creeping into the fridge and sampling them! This recipe gives enough chocolate to be able to dip the fruits completely, so reduce the amount if you will only half-dip them.

16 strawberries	8-10 apple slices
8-10 cherries	350 g (12 oz) good-quality dark chocolate
8-10 grapes	
8-10 tangerine segments	

SERVES 8 SENSIBLE PEOPLE OR 4 GLUTTONS

Melt the chocolate in a bowl over some hot water then, using a cocktail stick, dip each piece of fruit into the chocolate. Line a baking sheet with greaseproof paper and place the chocolate-dipped fruits on to it. Alternatively, you could leave the piece of fruit on the cocktail stick and imbed it in half a cabbage or grapefruit until the chocolate has set.

Once the chocolate has set, place the fruits on a suitable serving dish and keep in the refrigerator. Eat fairly soon after making, and do not leave overnight (not much chance in this house!)

DEVON CREAM TRUFFLES WITH ELDERBERRY WINE

You could either serve these with the Chocolate Dipped Fruits or, having had those with the Mango Heaven, these could be served with coffee. They are scrumptious but one or two each is usually enough unless you have a chocaholic among the party.

50 ml (2 fl oz) double cream	25 ml (1 fl oz) elderberry wine (or your own choice of alcohol)
50 g (2 oz) butter at room temperature	powdered drinking chocolate, cocoa powder or chopped nuts for decoration
175 g (6 oz) good-quality dark chocolate	

━━━━ MAKES ABOUT 24 TRUFFLES ━━━━

Reduce the cream by boiling it in a heavy-based pan for a few minutes. Lower the heat and stir in the chocolate (broken into small pieces) and the elderberry wine. Keep stirring until the chocolate has melted, then add the butter. Once the mixture is smooth, pour it into a dish and leave in the refrigerator until firm.

Using a teaspoon, shape the mixture into balls and roll in powdered drinking chocolate, cocoa powder or chopped nuts. Keep in the refrigerator until about 10 minutes before serving.

DRINKS PARTIES

Parties where the emphasis is on conversation, with drinks and only a little food, can be an excellent way to entertain large numbers of people whom you could not seat around a dining table. If you get all the food organized before the arrival of the guests, and have some extra helpers to dispense the drinks, then in theory you should be able to have fun and talk to the guests.

Serving unusual non-alcoholic drinks is important, because otherwise teetotallers and drivers will feel hard-done-by and excluded. I usually allow about 8-10 nibbles per person, depending on the time of day that the party is being held and the tastiness of the nibbles.

Talk nicely to your wine merchant and he or she will probably lend you the glasses free of charge. (Assuming you have bought the drink there, of course. A friend of mine asked for a free loan of her wine merchant's glasses and couldn't understand why he was rather brusque when she said she would be buying the wine from the supermarket because it was cheaper!) Have a really good collection of paper napkins dotted around the room or area that you are using as it is very embarrassing for guests when they have sticky fingers and can't wipe them on anything.

LYCHEES STUFFED WITH BRANDIED CHICKEN

These are delicious and unusual titbits that have most people coming back for more. You can always vary the filling to ring the changes.

3 skinned chicken breasts	50 ml (2 fl oz) oil
30 ml (2 tbsp) cognac	30 ml (2 tbsp) soy sauce
	50 g (2 oz) apple purée
10 g (2 tsp) finely grated fresh ginger root	6 × 500 g (1 lb 2 oz) cans of lychees
50 g (2 oz) butter	salt and black pepper

———— MAKES ABOUT 60 ————

Melt the butter in a frying pan and add the oil and fresh ginger. Slice the chicken breasts and sauté until thoroughly cooked through. Place the entire contents of the frying pan in the bowl of a food processor and add all the remaining ingredients except the lychees. Process thoroughly until you have a smooth paste.

Drain the lychees well, particularly the cavities left by the stones. Fill a piping bag, using a small plain nozzle, and pipe a little of the chicken mixture into each lychee. Place them all on a lightly greased baking sheet and thoroughly warm through in the oven before serving.

FILO TRIANGLES WITH MUSHROOMS, WALNUTS AND MOZZARELLA

These usually disappear like lightning and are very simple to make. You can use other cheeses or nuts if you wish.

275 g (10 oz) grated Mozzarella cheese	100 ml (4 fl oz) white wine
500 g (1 lb 2 oz) button mushrooms	10 ml (2 tsp) lemon juice
225 g (8 oz) finely chopped walnuts	10 g (2 tsp) finely chopped chives
50 g (2 oz) butter	700 g (1 lb 8 oz) filo pastry
100 g (4 oz) chopped onion	175 g (6 oz) butter for pastry
50 g (2 oz) finely chopped parsley	salt and pepper

———— MAKES ABOUT 60-70 ————

Melt the 50 g (2 oz) of butter in a pan and add the onion, salt, pepper and chives. Cook gently until the onion is transparent. Chop the mushrooms, then add them to the onions and cook until tender. If the mushrooms make quite a lot of liquid, remove most of the solids and boil the liquid hard until it is reduced. Add the wine and reduce again. Add the lemon juice and parsley.

Pour into a mixing bowl and leave to cool, then stir in the grated Mozzarella cheese and walnuts. Melt the 175 g (6 oz) of butter. Unwrap the filo pastry sheets and cover any that you are not using with a damp cloth. Cut the sheets into strips about 12.5 cm (5 in) wide, then work with one sheet at a time. Brush with butter and fold in half lengthwise. Brush the top with butter and place about 10 g (2 tsp) of the filling at the end of the strip and fold across as shown in the diagram. Repeat with the rest of the filo pastry and filling. Put the triangles on a greased baking sheet and brush lightly with butter. Cook in a pre-heated oven at 190°C (375°F), Gas Mark 5 for about 20 minutes until golden. Serve warm.

WHEN MAKING FOOD FOR A DRINKS PARTY, SIZE IS OF THE ESSENCE: SMALL IS BEAUTIFUL. GUESTS WILL BE WARY OF HELPING THEMSELVES TO ANYTHING THAT LOOKS TRICKY TO EAT OR IS TOO LARGE TO BE MANAGED IN MORE THAN A COUPLE OF MOUTHFULS. THESE FILO TRIANGLES WITH MUSHROOMS, WALNUTS AND MOZZARELLA, AND LYCHEES STUFFED WITH BRANDIED CHICKEN, FIT THE BILL PERFECTLY.

THIS DIAGRAM SHOWS HOW TO FOLD UP THE FILO PASTRY TO MAKE THE TRIANGLES.

CHERRY TOMATOES WITH TAPENADE

Although rather fiddly to make these tomatoes look impressive and are always popular. They're also good starters for a dinner party.

THESE STUFFED TOMATOES HAVE A WONDERFULLY MEDITERRANEAN FLAVOUR, SO ARE ESPECIALLY GOOD FOR SUMMER PARTIES.

60 cherry tomatoes	45 ml (3 tbsp) virgin olive oil
450 g (1 lb) black olives	
100 g (4 oz) green olives	150 ml (¼ pint) good mayonnaise
5 g (1 tsp) minced garlic	
4 tinned anchovy fillets	sprig of fresh thyme
10 ml (2 tbsp) dark rum	parsley or coriander leaves for decoration

━━ MAKES 60 ━━

Remove the stones from the black and green olives. Put all the ingredients, except the tomatoes and the mayonnaise, in a food processor or blender and process until you have a smooth paste. If you do not have a food processor you can chop the olives, anchovies and thyme fincly by hand. Add a little of the mayonnaise and stir well or process for a couple of seconds. Taste and then add more mayonnaise if the mixture is too strong for you.

Wash and dry the tomatoes. Slice a little from the top of each one and, using a small melon baller, carefully remove the contents of the tomatoes and discard. Sprinkle the insides with a little salt, pepper and sugar, and place upside down on a wire rack to drain for an hour or so. Fill a piping bag with the tapenade and use it to stuff the tomatoes. Garnish each one with a small green leaf, such as parsley or coriander.

SPICED FRUIT COOLER

I think this recipe is a very good reason for giving alcohol a miss; it's much nicer than some wines I've drunk in the past!

1.8 litres (3 pints) sparkling mineral water	10 cloves
	175 g (6 oz) sugar
1.8 litres (3 pints) fresh orange juice	450 ml (¾ pint) water
900 ml (1½ pints) fresh grapefruit juice	275 g (10 oz) runny honey
	1 orange for decoration
900 ml (1½ pints) fresh lemon juice	1 lemon for decoration
2 cinnamon sticks	ice cubes for decoration

━━ SERVES ABOUT 50 GLASSES ━━

Thoroughly chill all the fruit juices and the mineral water. Mix the 450 ml (¾ pint) of water, cinnamon sticks, cloves and sugar in a pan and bring to the boil. Stir gently until all the sugar has dissolved. Simmer for about 5 minutes, then add the honey, stirring until it has dissolved. Remove from the heat and leave to cool.

Once the mixture has cooled, strain it into a large punch bowl (preferably the most attractive one you can find), and add the fruit juices and the sparkling mineral water. Stir gently. Decorate with slices of orange and lemon and ice cubes.

STRAWBERRY SUMMER CUP

Having said how much I like that last recipe, I have to admit that, provided I'm not driving, this summer cup is out of this world. Beware when sampling it – I've known people to drink very large quantities of this because it is so wonderful.

300 ml (½ pint) Grand Marnier liqueur	2 kg (4½ lb) ripe strawberries
300 ml (½ pint) Kirsch liqueur	6 oranges
4-5 litres (7-8 pints) medium-dry white wine	
SERVES ABOUT 45/50 GLASSES	

Slice the oranges and strawberries, then place in a large bowl and pour over the Grand Marnier and Kirsch liqueurs. If possible, place in a refrigerator and leave to soak for about 1 hour, but not much longer or the fruit will be past its best. Then pour over the wine and stir the mixture well.

ADDICTIVE MELON COOLER

The name says it all. Addictive it certainly is, because it's quite delectable and tastes very innocent – take care!

6 large honeydew melons	crushed ice
5-6 litres (9-10 pints) dry white wine	borage or mint leaves for decoration
300 ml (½ pint) grenadine syrup	
SERVES ABOUT 45/50 GLASSES	

Place batches of the melon, grenadine and a little wine in a food processor or blender. Process for a few seconds until the mixture is smooth. Repeat until all the melon has been liquidized. Place the melon and grenadine concoction in a large bowl, add the remaining wine and a heap of crushed ice. Stir well and decorate with plenty of borage or mint leaves.

THE DRIED VARIETY CAN NEVER BEAT THE TASTE AND COLOUR OF FRESH HERBS, AND SOMETIMES THEY GIVE YOU A BONUS OF LOVELY FLOWERS TOO, LIKE THIS BORAGE.

SMOKED SALMON PARCELS WITH LEMON CHEESE

Anything with smoked salmon always seems to be a winner at cocktail or drinks parties and this recipe is no exception. I find it very difficult not to nibble a few parcels while I prepare them.

30 slices of smoked salmon	salt and lots of black pepper
350 g (12 oz) cream cheese	cucumber sticks for decoration
2 lemons	celery leaves for decoration

——— MAKES ABOUT 60 ———

Grate the zest from the two lemons, then squeeze one of the lemons. Place this juice and all the zest in a small bowl and add the cream cheese. Stir thoroughly until they are completely combined. (It's much quicker to do this in a food processor.) If necessary, use some of the juice from the second lemon to make the cheese a soft paste that holds its shape.

Cut the slices of salmon in two or three, depending on their size, and place some lemon cheese at the end of each slice. Season well with lots of black pepper and a little salt if you wish. Roll up each slice and secure with a cocktail stick if necessary. Serve garnished with cucumber sticks and celery leaves.

I THINK SMOKED SALMON IS ONE OF LIFE'S GREAT PLEASURES, SO I ALWAYS ENJOY SERVING IT TO MY GUESTS. THESE SMOKED SALMON PARCELS WITH LEMON CHEESE CAN BE MADE VERY QUICKLY AND, ODDLY ENOUGH, THEY ALWAYS SEEM TO VANISH WITH EQUAL SPEED!

CHRISTMAS CELEBRATIONS

Christmas is one of the happiest times of year for me. It is a real family occasion, and we are lucky enough to be a happy family which thoroughly enjoys a large get-together where the ages range from 6 to 96. There are always stresses and strains at this time of year but most of them can be coped with and happy memories are made to be carried away once Christmas is over. Although Christmas is probably a time for children it doesn't take much effort to make it a happy time for adults as well. Quite apart from the food and drink, seeing friends and telephoning people you have not seen for ages can make the festive season very special.

There is a saying that you only get out of life what you put in, and Christmas illustrates that point very well. If you approach the occasion with a negative feeling of 'Oh no, not Christmas again', then it's likely to be as boring and unrewarding as you make it. I find the more effort we make, the more we feel our Christmas has been a real success after the festive season is over. Little things mean a lot and spending large amounts of money on lavish presents is not what Christmas is all about. Giving time and trouble instead is far more rewarding, both for the recipient of the gift and the giver.

Making most or all of your Christmas presents may sound like a lot of work, but it usually brings tremendous gratitude and enthusiasm when everyone unwraps their gifts and appreciates how much effort has gone into them. If you have a grumpy old uncle who is never happy, why not look on his Christmas present as a challenge rather than a chore, and make him something he will love, such as some home-made truffles or a jar of whisky marmalade? But even if you can't spare the time to make the presents yourself, you can still cook up a super meal that will please everyone and create the basis for a lovely and memorable day.

SOUTH WEST ENGLAND, WHERE WE LIVE, IS RENOWNED FOR ITS MILD CLIMATE, BUT I DO ENJOY THOSE CRISP, COLD MORNINGS WHEN EVERYTHING SPARKLES WITH HOAR FROST.

CHESTNUT AND BLACK CHERRY SOUP

This is quite an unusual soup but is always very popular. Don't serve giant bowlfuls as there are many more goodies to follow unless, of course, you've had a disaster and the rest of the meal has been consigned to the dustbin the colour of charcoal, because you were too busy talking and not concentrating on the cooking. Don't laugh, it happened!
The chestnuts and red wine give this soup an air of tradition, while the cherries provide an extra touch of sweetness. The soup can be made in advance.

1 × 425 g (15 oz) tin black cherries	150 ml (¼ pint) red wine
1.8 litres (3 pints) rich vegetable or chicken stock	45 ml (3 tbsp) brandy
	salt and black pepper
900 g (2 lb) fresh chestnuts	pinch of ground allspice
	garlic *croûtons* for decoration
45 g (3 tbsp) unsalted butter	
	finely chopped parsley for decoration
45 g (3 tbsp) flour	

━━━ SERVES ABOUT 8 ━━━

Drain the cherries and remove all the stones. Score a cross on each chestnut and then bake in a pre-heated oven for about 20 minutes at 190°C (375°F), Gas Mark 5. Test whether the chestnuts are ready by piercing them with a skewer – if it travels through the nuts easily, they are cooked. Peel the chestnuts and put them through a mincer or food processor until they are fine crumbs.

Simmer the stock, chestnuts and cherries in a pan for 25 minutes. In a slightly larger pan, melt the butter and add the flour. Stirring continuously, cook for 5-10 minutes. Add the stock, chestnut and cherry mixture to the roux (butter and flour) a little at a time, whisking vigorously with a wire balloon whisk as you add the liquid. Once the ingredients are well combined, with no

THERE IS SOMETHING
VERY RICH AND FESTIVE
ABOUT THIS CHESTNUT
AND BLACK CHERRY
SOUP, AND ALTHOUGH IT
IS QUITE TIME-CONSUMING
TO MAKE, THE END
RESULT IS WELL WORTH
THE TROUBLE.

lumps, add the brandy, red wine and seasonings.

Simmer for another 10 minutes. Alternatively, you may leave the soup at this stage and heat it up until it simmers when you are ready to serve it. Serve hot with garlic *croûtons* and finely chopped parsley sprinkled on to the soup.

POUSSIN WITH PECAN AND BOURBON STUFFING

Poussin makes a change from turkey, but if you wanted to stick to the traditional bird you could still use this stuffing.

8 tiny poussin	15 g (1 tbsp) finely chopped parsley
450 g (1 lb) shelled pecan nuts	15 g (1 tbsp) finely chopped mint
225 g (8 oz) mixed walnuts and cashew nuts	7 g (½ tbsp) finely chopped thyme
350 g (¾ lb) dried prunes	7 g (½ tbsp) finely chopped sage
75 g (3 oz) sultanas	50 g (2 oz) butter
225 g (8 oz) dried apricots	3 pears, peeled, cored and chopped
300 ml (½ pint) orange juice	2 apples, peeled, cored and chopped
100 g (4 oz) minced pork	150 ml (¼ pint) Bourbon whiskey
100 g (4 oz) minced veal or chicken	sunflower oil
7 g (½ tbsp) fresh rosemary needles	
SERVES 8	

Rinse the poussin inside and out and pat dry with kitchen paper. Using a teaspoon, carefully fill the cavities of each poussin with the stuffing. Pack it in as tightly as you can and then place the poussin in a large roasting dish. Drizzle a little sunflower oil over each bird and cook in a pre-heated oven for 30 minutes at 180°C (350°F), Gas Mark 4. Cook the leftover stuffing in the oven in a small cake or roasting tin with the poussin and serve separately.

RICH CHICKEN AND CRANBERRY GRAVY

This lovely gravy can be served at other times of the year with chicken breast fillets.

1 litre (1¾ pints) strong chicken stock	1 small onion
150 ml (¼ pint) sieved cranberry juice	10 g (2 tsp) butter
150 ml (¼ pint) red wine	salt and black pepper
SERVES 8	

Place all the dried fruit in a pan with the orange juice and heat gently, then leave to soak overnight. Melt the butter in a frying pan and add all the minced meat and fresh herbs. Cook until all traces of pink disappear from the meat. Drain the dried fruits and chop them roughly. Place in a large mixing bowl and add the meat and herb mixture. Add the chopped pears and apples, the nuts and Bourbon and mix well, then put to one side.

Chop the onion as finely as possible or process in a food processor. Fry in a saucepan with the butter until lightly browned, then add the chicken stock and boil rapidly. When the liquid is reduced by about a third, stir in the cranberry juice and red wine. Season with salt and pepper to taste. If you want the gravy to be a little thicker, you can either reduce the liquid by boiling it again or add some flour mixed with butter, and stir well until the gravy has thickened.

MINIATURE STUFFED POTATOES

These received a five-star rating from my family when I first served them, and have been requested many times since throughout the year.

24 small potatoes, about 4-5 cm (1½-2 in) in diameter	25 g (1 oz) roughly chopped parsley
	25 g (1 oz) fresh dill
225 g (8 oz) cream cheese	1 spring onion
	15 ml (1 tbsp) double cream
salt and black pepper	
25 g (1 oz) roughly chopped watercress	

SERVES 8

Place the scrubbed but unpeeled potatoes in a roasting dish in a pre-heated oven, at 200°C (400°F), Gas Mark 6, and bake for about 40 minutes or until they are soft when pierced with a skewer. While they are cooking, mix the cream cheese with the double cream. Chop the herbs and spring onion in a food processor, as finely as possible, and then add the cream cheese and double cream mixture. Process until well blended. If you do not have a food processor then chop the herbs and onion as best you can and add the cheese and cream. Season to taste.

Fill a piping bag with the cheese and herb mixture. Slice down the middle of each potato without completely cutting it in half, and then sandwich it back together by piping a generous amount of the cheese and herb mixture between the two halves. Serve as soon as possible.

PEAR AND CINNAMON BREW

I prefer to stay sober when I have a meal to cook – see my comments for Chestnut and Black Cherry Soup! But not drinking much alcohol doesn't mean that you have to miss out on the fun. This is a delicious drink that might well be chosen by serious drinkers or teetotallers alike.

75 cl (1 bottle) pear cider	5 crushed cinnamon sticks
300 ml (½ pint) apple juice	50 g (2 oz) demerara sugar
12 whole cloves	8 whole cinnamon sticks
6 whole allspice berries	

———— SERVES 8 DRIVERS! ————

Cut out a piece of muslin, about 17.5 cm (7 in) in diameter, and place the cloves, allspice and crushed cinnamon sticks in the middle of it. Tie up with string. Place all the remaining ingredients, and the bag of spices, in a pan and simmer gently for 10-20 minutes. Remove the bag of spices and serve with a whole cinnamon stick for each person. Remember to use strong glasses or mugs that can withstand the heat.

MUSHROOM AND MADEIRA BAKE

Although this is intended to be a vegetarian alternative, it is also very popular with meat-eaters. Even my daughter Pippa rates this very highly and we now have it quite often as a family supper dish.

100 g (4 oz) cashew nuts	450 g (1 lb) mushrooms
100 g (4 oz) walnuts	450 g (1 lb) granary breadcrumbs
100 g (4 oz) unsalted butter	450 g (1 lb) fresh tomatoes
30 ml (2 tbsp) sunflower oil	60 ml (4 tbsp) Madeira
2 large onions	salt and black pepper

———— SERVES 8 ————

Chop or process the nuts and mix them with the breadcrumbs. Melt the butter in a frying pan and gently fry the breadcrumb and nut mixture until it is pale gold in colour. Remove from the pan and set aside. Chop the onions, mushrooms and tomatoes coarsely and fry in the pan with the oil. Once they have softened a little, stir in the Madeira and continue to cook gently. Add plenty of freshly ground black pepper and a little salt to taste.

Lightly grease an ovenproof dish and put a thin layer of breadcrumb mix on the bottom. Carefully pile the vegetable mixture

over the top and level it out. Then put the remaining breadcrumb mix on top. Sprinkle the top of the mix with a little extra Madeira and bake in a pre-heated oven at 200°C (400°F), Gas Mark 6 for about 20-25 minutes or until golden brown.

LETHAL CHRISTMAS PUDDING

The Christmas pudding brought into the dining room with flames licking around its base is a very traditional and exciting climax to the Christmas meal. Using Calvados instead of normal brandy has worked well for years, including one year at a friend's house when she was rather too generous with the Calvados and it refused to be put out!

100 g (4 oz) currants	5 g (1 tsp) ground allspice
175 g (6 oz) sultanas	2 large free-range eggs
175 g (6 oz) raisins	100 g (4 oz) melted butter
juice and rind of 1 orange	30 ml (2 tbsp) brandy
juice and rind of 1 lime	45 ml (3 tbsp) port
50 g (2 oz) dark brown sugar	45 ml (3 tbsp) Calvados
50 g (2 oz) chopped walnuts	150 ml (¼ pint) brandy for adding later
175 g (6 oz) granary breadcrumbs	300 ml (½ pint) Calvados for serving

═══════ SERVES 8 ═══════

Combine the grated orange and lime rinds, breadcrumbs, walnuts, allspice and brown sugar with the dried fruits. In a separate bowl, whisk together the orange and lime juice, melted butter, eggs and alcohol. Do not add the large amounts of brandy and Calvados at this stage. Stir the two mixtures together until well combined.

Butter a 1.2 litre (2 pint) pudding basin and pour the mixture into it. Leave to stand for half an hour, then cover with a double layer of well-buttered greaseproof paper and secure it around the basin with string. Take a large piece of muslin and wrap a

double thickness around the pudding basin and again secure with string or tie in a knot at the top.

Half-fill a very large saucepan with water. Place the pudding basin inside, keeping its top clear of the water, and steam for between 7-8 hours. The saucepan must never be allowed to boil dry. Once the time is up, remove the pudding and leave it wrapped until it is completely cool, then remove the muslin and greaseproof paper. Using a skewer or knitting needle, make some holes in the top of the pudding and pour over about 75 ml (3 fl oz) of the remaining brandy. Wrap the pudding securely in buttered greaseproof paper and aluminium foil and store in a cool place.

Approximately one month later, open the pudding and, using the same skewer technique, pour the remaining 75 ml (3 fl oz) of brandy over the pudding and wrap it up again securely. The pudding will keep for up to 1 year in a cool place. I usually make mine in about October, so the second dose of brandy is administered about a month before Christmas.

To serve the pudding, either steam it for

FOR MANY PEOPLE CHRISTMAS DINNER WOULD BE INCOMPLETE WITHOUT THE TRADITIONAL PUDDING. FOR MAXIMUM FLAVOUR, IT IS BEST MADE A COUPLE OF MONTHS IN ADVANCE AND LEFT TO MATURE, WITH THE HELP OF A GENEROUS TOT OR TWO OF BRANDY.

FILO WATERLILIES WITH FIGGY MINCEMEAT

If you fancy making a slight break from tradition why not try these? They are an unusual alternative to the standard mince pie and I personally prefer filo to shortcrust pastry. Try them and see what you think.

MINCEMEAT	
225 g (8 oz) dried figs	25 g (1 oz) unsalted butter
75 g (3 oz) pecan nuts	5 g (1 tsp) ground allspice
350 g (12 oz) cooking apples (preferably Bramleys)	2 g (½ tsp) ground nutmeg
75 ml (3 fl oz) Calvados	2 g (½ tsp) ground cinnamon
50 g (2 oz) stem ginger in syrup	
675 g (1½ lb) mixed dried fruit	

FILO PASTRY WATERLILIES	
approximately 20 sheets filo pastry	225 g (8 oz) melted butter

SERVES ABOUT 8

To make the mincemeat, put the mixed dried fruit in a bowl and pour over the Calvados, then leave to soak in a warm place for several hours. Peel, core and chop the apples, and mince or process them together with the stem ginger, pecan nuts and figs. If using a food processor you may need to add more Calvados to moisten the mixture.

Add the remaining ingredients and stir really well to make sure they are well combined. Put into clean jars and seal. Do not keep too long (chance would be a fine thing in this house!); I would suggest 6-8 weeks in the refrigerator at the most.

Using good kitchen scissors, cut the pastry into 5-5.75 cm (2-2½ in) squares (cut a stack of sheets at once, not one sheet at a time). Keep the filo pastry covered with a clean damp cloth as much as possible to avoid it drying out. Butter a nine-hole bun tin and place a square of pastry over one hole. Brush the top of the pastry with melted butter and cover with another square of

ABOVE: OLD MAN'S BEARD, OR *CLEMATIS VITALBA,* LOOKS EVEN MORE MAGICAL WHEN INTERWOVEN WITH SPANGLED GOLD THREADS. TAKE CARE IF YOU WILL BE PLACING LIGHTED CANDLES NEARBY, BECAUSE IT IS HIGHLY FLAMMABLE. FACING PAGE: MULLED WINE, VICTORIA FARM STYLE, IS A GOOD PRE-DINNER DRINK, GUARANTEED TO PUT EVERYONE IN A SUITABLY FESTIVE MOOD.

about 2-3 hours or, if you have a microwave oven, cook it for 5 minutes on high and then allow it to stand for a further 5 minutes. (Remove the aluminium foil first if you are microwaving the pudding.) Once the pudding has been reheated, place it on a decorative serving dish, warm the 300 ml (½ pint) of Calvados and pour it over the pudding so that a small puddle accumulates all round the bottom. Place a sprig of holly in the top and set light to the Calvados. Take care: this is not called Lethal Christmas Pudding for the amount of alcohol involved so much as for the spectacular flames of the Calvados! Serve with cream, custard, brandy or rum butter – or all of them . . .

THIS DIAGRAM SHOWS THE
FIVE FILO PASTRY
SQUARES ARRANGED TO
GIVE A PETALLED EFFECT.

pastry, placing this second square at right angles to the first. Continue to layer about five pieces of pastry, buttering between each layer and placing the corners of the squares in different positions each time to give a petalled effect (see diagram). Fill each pastry case with between 10-15 g (1 dsp to 1 tbsp) of mincemeat and bake in a pre-heated oven at 160°C (325°F), Gas Mark 3 for about 45 minutes.

MULLED WINE – VICTORIA FARM STYLE

The aroma of this mulled wine sums up Christmas for me. It is quite strong, so ideal for prim and proper relatives or friends who need to feel relaxed before they can join in the fun.

75 cl (1 bottle) claret	7 g (1 heaped tsp) mixed spice
150 ml (¼ pint) unsweetened orange juice	2 large juicy oranges, each cut into eight pieces
150 ml (¼ pint) water	
150 ml (¼ pint) port	8 cinnamon sticks
50 g (2 oz) brown sugar	

SERVES 8 NON-DRIVERS!

Put all the ingredients, except the cinnamon sticks, in a saucepan and place on a very low heat. Gently warm the mull for an hour or so. If you want to prepare it in advance you can warm it for an hour, leave it to cool and then reheat it when it is needed. Serve in very tough glasses or mugs, with cinnamon sticks as stirrers. Do not include any of the pieces of orange as they have an embarrassing habit of falling on to your nose as you try to drink the wine.

CHILDREN'S PARTIES

I have very happy memories of birthday parties from my childhood, with fancy dress and wonderful cakes, parcels and games. I'm not sure that my daughter will have so many memories because I haven't organized as many parties for her as my mother did for me. There is a tremendous pressure today to have expensive entertainers or flashy trips to somewhere special, and in trying to outdo each other I think the children have missed out on a lot of fun. A well organized, straightforward party, with no entertainer but just popular games (preferably held outside) and food that the children really like, can be a marvellous recipe for success.

Having said that, it does mean that the parents need plenty of fun and enthusiasm and I realize that not everyone wants to spend a precious Saturday afternoon with 20 children belonging to other people. If the idea appeals to you, however, then read on!

We're back to lists again. I make copious lists, timetables of which game is to be played when and buy double the number of prizes that I think I'll need, and all that seems to work. If possible, each child should win something at some point (this may call for considerable ingenuity at times). Ask some of your friends to help, so that when a particularly irritating child is pushing his or her luck, you can call on some back-up troops to stop you doing anything you might regret later.

As a final tip, one riotous success was when several of the fathers got together and gave a cabaret dressed in silly clothes. This worked on two counts; not only did the children think it was hilarious seeing grown men dressed up and looking silly, but the fact it was their father or their friend's father seemed to add tremendously to the hilarity of the occasion. If they're honest, I think the dads had a good laugh as well.

MINI CHEESE AND TOMATO PIZZAS

Pizza has become a firm favourite with children now and these mini pizzas mean they are not faced with a large portion that they cannot finish. Beware – they also make good missiles if things get out of hand!

900 g (2 lb) plain flour	675 g (1½ lb) Mozzarella cheese
25 g (1 oz) fresh yeast	
450 ml (¾ pint) water	225 g (8 oz) grated Parmesan cheese
5 g (1 tsp) salt	
900 g (2 lb) tomatoes	180 ml (12 tbsp) oil
	salt and pepper to taste

SERVES 20

Sift the flour into a bowl, make a well in the centre and crumble the fresh yeast into the well. Pour over about 100 ml (4 fl oz) of the water, mix a little of the flour with the water and yeast and leave for 10 minutes. Then stir well to incorporate all the remaining flour, and add the rest of the water and salt. Beat until light. Divide the dough into four pieces, shape into balls and leave in the refrigerator for 1-2 hours.

Brush two large baking sheets with oil and put in the oven to heat at 220°C (425°F), Gas Mark 7. Roll out the dough (using a floured rolling pin) into a circle, making sure it is fairly thin. Using a smooth-edged biscuit cutter, cut out as many circles as possible. Repeat with the rest of the dough. The number of circles you cut out of the mixture will depend on the size of cutter you choose.

Arrange the dough bases on the hot baking sheets. Slice the Mozzarella cheese and arrange it on the dough bases. Peel and slice the tomatoes and place them on top of the cheese slices. Season well with salt and pepper and sprinkle a little Parmesan on top and then, with a teaspoon, dribble a little oil over each pizza. Bake in the oven for 10 minutes or so, but keep an eye on them as they should not be too well done. If you are intending to reheat them later, then make sure they are underdone as children shy away from eating anything that looks vaguely burnt.

MINI HOT DOGS WITH SWEET ONIONS

These are another favourite of most children, but are scaled down in size so they will have room for some of the other goodies as well.

20 tiny bridge rolls	30 ml (2 tbsp) tomato ketchup
10 frankfurters	
2 large onions	15 g (1 tbsp) sugar
	30 g (2 tbsp) oil

SERVES 20

Peel and finely slice the onions and separate into rings. Heat the oil in a frying pan and sauté the onions gently until they are tender. Sprinkle the sugar into the pan and cook

CHILDREN ARE VERY
CONSERVATIVE ABOUT
WHAT THEY WILL AND
WILL NOT EAT. I'VE FOUND
THE BEST BET FOR
CHILDREN'S PARTIES IS TO
MAKE THE FOOD LOOK
FUN TO EAT, AND ALSO TO
KEEP THE PORTIONS
SMALL, AS I HAVE DONE
HERE WITH THESE MINI
HOT DOGS WITH SWEET
ONIONS AND MINI CHEESE
AND TOMATO PIZZAS.

until it dissolves, then add the tomato ketchup and stir well.

Heat the frankfurters in boiling water. To make up the hot dogs, slice the rolls and put half a frankfurter inside each one. Serve the tomato and onion mixture on top or, to play safe, separately in a dish with a spoon so the children can help themselves.

**AND TEDDY CAME TOO ...
GIVE YOUR CHILD'S
FAVOURITE SOFT TOY A
RINGSIDE SEAT, BUT
PREFERABLY OUT OF THE
WAY OF STICKY OR
INQUISITIVE FINGERS.**

MINI PITTA BREADS WITH CHEESE AND APPLE CUBES

I have chosen mini pitta breads because children much prefer eating several small items to one large helping.

20 miniature pitta breads	lemon juice
75 g (3 oz) mildest Cheddar cheese	tomato ketchup
	mayonnaise
5 sweet eating apples	sweet pickle

──── SERVES 20 ────

Chop the Cheddar cheese into small cubes. Peel and core the apple and chop into small cubes, then brush with lemon juice to prevent them going brown. Arrange on the table with a central plate of pitta breads and then small bowls of the other ingredients in a circle around the plate. The children can then mix their own concoctions from the bowls of cheese, apple, tomato ketchup, mayonnaise and sweet pickle.

HOME-MADE CRISPS WITH TOMATO DIP

The home-made variety do taste better than bought crisps, and it is a source of fascination to children that mothers can actually make something as clever as crisps: my nephews were very impressed with their mother's efforts. Do make these on the day they are to be eaten because they really don't keep very well.

10-12 large baking potatoes	100 ml (4 fl oz) tomato ketchup
vegetable oil for deep frying	100 ml (4 fl oz) good mayonnaise
	salt

──── SERVES 20 ────

Slice the potatoes thinly, about 3 mm (⅛ in) thick. This is easiest if you have a

special slicer or mandolin, but you can use a sharp knife instead if necessary. Put the slices in cold water until needed.

Heat a pan with vegetable oil – do not fill it more than half to two-thirds full. Alternatively, you can use a deep-fat fryer. Drain the slices of potato and dry well. Deep-fry them until golden and crisp, then drain and sprinkle lightly with salt.

Mix together the tomato ketchup and mayonnaise and serve in a small bowl surrounded by the potato crisps.

CHILDREN ADORE BOLD COLOURS, AND THESE VIVID TULIPS WOULD SET THE TONE FOR ANY PARTY.

CHOCOLATE CRUNCHIES

What can I say about these perennial favourites? I usually make twice this amount, as the parents like them too and leftovers never last more than a day or so.

225 g (8 oz) good-quality plain chocolate	10 g (2 tsp) butter
	175 g (6 oz) cornflakes

SERVES 20 OR SO, DEPENDING ON THEIR POPULARITY

Melt the chocolate and butter in a bowl over some hot water. Once the chocolate has melted, add the cornflakes. Using a metal spoon, turn the cornflakes gently but thoroughly in the chocolate until they are all evenly covered. Spoon heaped tablespoons into paper cases and cool, preferably in the refrigerator, until set.

THE ANIMAL'S BEDROOM

The birthday cake is often the centrepiece of a children's party and in my experience is the criterion upon which little girls judge the ability of their friend's mother's catering. We have been through a host of ideas during Pippa's 11 birthdays, and animals have usually scored the highest marks, so this cake should give you plenty of inspiration. I am currently wrestling with the problem of making a row of Arab stallions in bed since horses are Pippa's greatest love (after guinea pigs).

DECORATING INGREDIENTS

450 g (1 lb) marzipan (ready-made or home-made)	thin cake board
	cake decorating tools
450 g (1 lb) sugarpaste (bought)	apricot jam
	royal icing
powdered food colouring	egg white

You can make as many beds as you like. I would suggest one for each year being celebrated, so one candle can go at the foot of each bed. However, if you are holding a party for a two-year old and inviting twenty guests, the cake would not be big enough to feed them all, so one bed could be made far more elaborate than all the others and the two candles placed by that bed. These ingredients make one bed, so multiply by however many beds you want to make.

You can use many different types of cake as a base for the bed. Chocolate is always popular, but Madeira or fruit cake is sturdy to work with. Make a batch of cake in a Swiss roll tin (which will give enough cake for several beds) and allow it to cool.

The cake board or base can be covered with coloured marzipan to give a carpeted effect. If you wish to do this, colour the marzipan first and then roll it out thinly. Attach the marzipan to the board by brushing a little egg white over the board before placing the sheet of marzipan over it.

Cut a slab of cake about 10 × 7.5 cm (4 × 3 in). Brush the top and sides with apricot jam. Roll out some marzipan and cover the top and sides of the cake with it. This makes the bed. To make the headboard, colour a piece of marzipan according to your colour scheme, roll it out and cut out a bedhead shape, either straight across or curved. Using the same marzipan, make some square or round poles to go each side of the bedhead. Leave to set for 2 days.

Using the sugarpaste, make one or two pillows for the bed. Attach the pillows and the bedhead to the cake base with a little royal icing. You also need to make a fake body shape to tuck inside the bed, but this need only be a sausage of sugarpaste. Colour some marzipan for the head and hands of the animal inside the bed.

As a general guide, the heads are made from small balls of marzipan and the ears are usually made separately and then stuck on with royal icing. The eyes are first marked with a cocktail stick and later piped on with some royal icing. Other features such as noses can also be piped on or made from

small pieces of marzipan. You also need to make two paws (or hands) to show over the quilt. Place the animal's head on the pillow and secure in position with a little egg white.

To make the sheet, roll out some white sugarpaste and make a cover large enough to drape over the top and sides of the bed. Place the sheet on the bed, slightly covering the bottom of the animal's face.

The quilt or bedspread is made by rolling out some sugarpaste, coloured according to your colour scheme. Cut it into a rectangle slightly smaller than the sheet and drape it over the bed. To decorate it, you can either use a cake decorator's embossing tool and press designs into the sugarpaste or, using edible colourings, you can paint designs on to the sugarpaste. The beds in this example have a selection of bed linen. Alternatively, you could leave the quilt quite plain.

Now add the finishing touches. The hands can be placed either side of the head, just peeping over the sheet. Then, using royal icing, pipe in the eyes and any other facial details needed that were not put on with marzipan. Other odds and ends, such as shoes, slippers, books, hot water bottles or miniature teddies, can also be made from marzipan or sugarpaste and painted. They can be held in place with a little royal icing.

THE APPEARANCE OF THE BIRTHDAY CAKE WILL BE SUBJECTED TO SOME HIGHLY CRITICAL APPRAISAL BY YOUR CHILD'S GUESTS, SO A CAKE OF THIS COMPLEXITY SHOULD WIN YOU PLENTY OF ADMIRATION!

GIFTS

Home-produced gifts, whether they come from your larder, garden or sewing box, are always greatly treasured. One of the easiest ways to please is to cook up some goodies in the kitchen and then to put them in an attractive presentation basket. You can make all manner of edible presents, and if you think about the recipient for a moment something he or she particularly likes will probably spring to mind. One of my friends (mentioning no names) is a self-confessed chocaholic, so finding a suitable present for her is easy – a basket of assorted chocolate cookies and other goodies is always received with grateful enthusiasm.

Pot-pourri is a popular gift but far more so if it is a really good quality mixture that you have made with flowers from your own garden and packaged beautifully. If you imagine where the recipient might display the pot-pourri, you can plan a suitable colour scheme. A collection of pot-pourri and soaps, bath salts and other scented luxuries can all be packaged in a lovely basket, swathed in cellophane and decorated with a large bow, to make a lavish gift. Of course, you can buy a commercial equivalent, but a personal collection specially made by you will be far more interesting and mean much more.

Making aromatic mixtures and using fragrance is an art that has been in practice for thousands of years. In many ways it was far more necessary then than it is today. We only use fragrance as a gentle accessory to waft through the house or softly perfume our linen or clothes, but in earlier times it may well have been the only way to mask some of the more intolerable smells! For example, during the winter months people smothered themselves in goose grease to keep warm, and went without their monthly (yes, that's right!) baths for the same reason. I can't imagine what they smelt like but perhaps it's better that way! We have progressed to carpets rather than sweet-smelling hay on our floors but, even so, pot-pourri adds an extra dimension to a room. A really pretty bowl of pot-pourri looks so attractive on a dressing table or in the bathroom; it can be colour co-ordinated with the decor of the room or given a special seasonal smell at Christmas, for example.

MAKING POT-POURRI

One of the most important factors when making your own pot-pourri is to ensure that the recipe includes an ingredient that will keep your mixture smelling strongly for some time. If you just use dried flower heads and a little perfumed oil without adding a fixative, the smell will be very fleeting. It can also be an expensive way of creating your own pot-pourri as the oil will need renewing very often indeed.

There are two really reliable fixatives to choose from. The most popular is dried orris root, which comes from the root of the iris plant. It is available in two forms, either powdered or in a cut form which resembles gravel or smallish lumps. The other possibility is calamus root which is also available in both forms, but I always use it in the cut form. Powdered fixative is ideal for making pot-pourri to fill small flat sachets that are to be tucked in drawers, between piles of linen and so on, but it is not suitable for large decorative bowls of pot-pourri because it coats the ingredients and leaves a dull, powdery finish on the plant materials.

Experimenting with pot-pourri

You can either grow your own ingredients for pot-pourri making or you can bulk out what you already have in your own garden (which you will then dry) by buying ready dried ingredients. (See the list of suppliers at the back of the book.) The fixatives, however, are not easy to grow yourself, so I would recommend that you buy them. Equally, the essential oils could be made at home but that would entail a tremendous amount of work and a considerable number of flowers, so I would suggest you buy your essential oils too.

Many books are full of pot-pourri recipes, and friends may also pass on their favourites, but I think the greatest fun comes from creating your own mixes. Start by following some recipes to give you an idea of the quantities and proportions that are used, and then experiment to produce something that is special to you.

Drying the plant material

Pot-pourri is made from dried flowers, seed heads and leaves, and if you have grown them yourself you will have to preserve them before following these recipes. The plant material can be dried in three ways – in air, in silica gel crystals which are bought from specialist suppliers and (although it sounds quite contradictory) in a mixture of equal parts of glycerine and water until the foliage changes colour.

Flowers dried in silica gel crystals look marvellous, but because this is a time-consuming and expensive method, it is best used only to dry flowers that are not suited to air drying or that will decorate the top of the pot-pourri. Fill the bottom of a clean plastic container, which has a close-fitting lid, with some of the crystals, arrange the flowers on them and then very gently spoon more crystals in and around the petals until they are completely buried. Replace the lid and leave for between two and four days, then test the flowers and remove if they are completely dry. The crystals can then be dried out in a low oven so they will be ready for use again.

Air drying your flowers and foliage is extremely simple and gives excellent results. Ideally, you should pick the flowers mid-morning, when the dew has evaporated but before the sun has become too hot. Arrange them in small bunches of no more than three or four stems, and hold them together with elastic bands. Don't be tempted to make up mixed bunches of flowers because some may take longer to dry than others, and cause problems as a result. The plant material must be dried in a warm, dark and airy place, so a roomy airing cupboard, provided it has adequate ventilation, is ideal. Hang the bunches by their stems, keeping them well apart from each other so plenty of air can circulate between them, and check them every few days. Most bunches take between a week and a month to dry, according to the thickness of their stems and the size of the flower heads. Only remove the bunches when you're sure they're completely dry, otherwise they could develop such nasty ailments as mildew, which won't do much to enhance the appearance or scent

of your carefully made pot-pourri!

You are unlikely to use all your dried material immediately, so will have to store it until it is needed. If you ask nicely, your local florist may give you some of the empty boxes that flowers arrive in from market, and these are ideal for storing dried flowers. Ensure the boxes are completely dry, tape over any ventilation holes (ideal doorways for picnicking insects), then line them with tissue paper and fill with the flowers. If you will only be using the heads of the flowers, you can remove the stems and store the flowers in shoe boxes to save space. Store the boxes, whether large or small, where they won't be damaged – placing them under the spare bed is often a good idea – and remember that the main enemies of dried flowers are damp, light and hungry insects and mice.

Preparing the fixative
At least two days before you start mixing up any of the recipes, you must combine your chosen fixative with your chosen essential oils and allow them to mature. Even though the recipes call for a selection of essential oils, you must mix up a separate quantity of each one with the fixative – these oil and fixative mixtures are then combined when you add the dried flowers.

ROSE PETALS ARE THE CLASSIC INGREDIENT FOR POT-POURRI, BUT TO OBTAIN THEM YOU DO HAVE TO DISMANTLE THE WHOLE ROSE HEAD. IF YOU HAVE A PARTICULARLY BEAUTIFUL ROSE YOU CAN PRESERVE ITS FLOWER HEADS INTACT IN SILICA GEL CRYSTALS RATHER THAN TEAR THEM APART, THEN USE THEM TO DECORATE THE TOP OF THE FINISHED POT-POURRI

In clean screw-top jars, mix up each essential oil and fixative in the ratio of approximately 175 drops (⅛ fl oz) of oil to every 50 g (2 oz) of orris or calamus root. Mix the two ingredients together well, screw on the lid and leave to mature. I usually leave my jars on the kitchen work-top and give them a good shake every time I walk past. This mixture will keep for a long time, so you can make it up in large quantities and store it for use at a later date. Do make sure you label each jar clearly because guessing which oil is in which jar is no fun after the first fifty sniffs.

Making up the recipe

Once the oil mixture has matured you are ready to make up a recipe. I have included some here for you to experiment with, but do remember you are the 'cook' and it is quite permissible to add anything you like, just as long as the oils you are using harmonize well. It really doesn't matter which dried flowers you use because they will have little scent by now, so choosing their colour and size is up to you. However, you must take care with the oils because mixing too many together doesn't always have a happy ending. When I first started experimenting

YOU DONT HAVE TO FOLLOW THESE POT-POURRI RECIPES TO THE LETTER; A WALK ROUND YOUR GARDEN (OR A GENEROUS FRIEND'S – BUT DO ASK FIRST) COULD REVEAL ALL SORTS OF FLOWERS THAT YOU CAN EXPERIMENT WITH AND USE INSTEAD.

with essential oils I got completely carried away, and managed to make one mixture that contained far too much oil of black pepper – you can imagine everyone's reaction when they sniffed it. It was a shame, and ruined some lovely fruit oils in the mixture. I often add a little black pepper to strawberries when I'm cooking, so I thought the same rule might apply to smells. Well, so it might I suppose if it is used very sparingly, but not the way I added it.

Measuring out the ingredients

The basic proportion is roughly one tablespoon of the root and oil mixture to one measure (I use 600 ml [1 pint]) of dried plant material. Once you have made up some trial batches, you can experiment with your own concoctions.

When you are working with dried materials to make up a pot-pourri, using a pair of kitchen scales to weigh every ingredient can be very irritating. I'm not very good about weighing things carefully for cookery recipes, so I'm certainly not inclined to spend ages weighing things out for pot-pourri. My main utensil for this job is an old 600 ml (1 pint) glass measuring jug which has been washed so many times that all the markings have rubbed off the sides. I dip this into a sack or bowlful of ingredients, measuring them by volume not weight – it's far quicker.

So seek out an old jug or large mug that you no longer use for cooking or drinking purposes and keep it as your pot-pourri measure. It's important not to use any piece of equipment that will later return to the kitchen because some plant materials are poisonous, the essential oils are very strong, and gravy tainted with jasmine oil is pretty revolting. (We know!) Collect together all the ingredients and equipment you need for your recipe before you begin, because it's very annoying to have to dash out and find an extra ingredient, and then start to enjoy yourself. Happy mixing!

PEACHES AND CREAM

3 measures peach rose-buds or petals	8 tablespoons calamus or orris root mixed with peach oil
2 measures cream globe amaranth flowers	2 tablespoons calamus or orris root mixed with sweet orange oil
2 measures pinky/peach *Helichrysum* flower heads	
3 measures cream rose petals	2 tablespoons calamus or orris root mixed with cinnamon oil
2 measures broken cinnamon sticks	

Prepare your calamus or orris root and oil mixtures at least two days before starting the recipe. Then mix all the ingredients together in a large bowl and store in one or more large containers. I have a collection of empty sweet jars which work well, but any large screw-topped containers will do. Keep these containers somewhere dark, so the contents won't fade, but accessible so that you can shake them regularly. Keep the mixture in the jars for at least 2-3 weeks, shaking them at intervals. You can then use the pot-pourri.

ROMANTIC ROSES

4 measures rose-buds and petals	1 measure cloves
4 measures larkspur flowers	8 tablespoons calamus or orris root with rose oil
1 measure rose leaves	2 tablespons calamus or orris root with lavender oil
1 measure silica dried pansies	
1 measure lavender flowers	2 tablespoons calamus or orris root mixed with allspice oil

Prepare the oil and fixative mixtures in advance, then mix all the ingredients together and store in large screw-top jars in a dark place. Shake the contents regularly for at least 2-3 weeks and then the pot-pourri may be used.

CHRISTMAS CHEER

2 measures costus flowers or baby pine cones	3 tablespoons calamus or orris root with pine oil
2 measures spruce or pine needles	2 tablespoons calamus or orris root with cinnamon oil
1 measure holly leaves	
1 measure mistletoe leaves	3 tablespoons calamus or orris root with sweet orange oil
2 measures broken cinnamon sticks	1 tablespoon calamus or orris root with clove oil
1 measure star anise	2 tablespoons calamus or orris root with rose oil
2 measures orange and lemon peel	

Prepare the oil and fixative mixtures in advance, then mix all the ingredients together and store in large screw-top jars in a dark place. Shake the contents regularly for at least 2-3 weeks and then the pot-pourri may be used.

Bathroom pot-pourri
There are many settings in the house that would be perfect for a bowl of pot-pourri, and one of my favourites is the bathroom. You can keep a large bowl of pot-pourri by itself in the bathroom or you can store small cakes of visitors' soaps in the pot-pourri, because they soon take on the fragrance. Here are two recipes that would be lovely for a bathroom or bedroom.

SEASIDE GARDEN

2 measures rose-buds or petals	5 tablespoons calamus or orris root with rose oil
2 measures lavender flowers	3 tablespoons calamus or orris root with lavender oil
2 measures peony petals	
2 measures silica dried pansies	2 tablespoons calamus or orris root with neroli (orange blossom) oil
2 measures sea shells or pearls	

WHEN LEAVING SOAPS IN BOWLS OF POT-POURRI TRY TO MATCH THE SMELL OF THE POT-POURRI TO THAT OF THE SOAPS IF THEY ARE ALREADY SCENTED.

Prepare the oil and fixative mixtures in advance, then mix all the ingredients together and store in large screw-top jars in a dark place. Shake them regularly during this time. Display with tiny soaps or by itself and decorated with silica dried roses or sprays of ribboned lavender.

STRAWBERRY POTS

2 measures pale pink globe amaranth flowers	½ measure bergamot leaves
2 measures pink rose-buds or petals	6 tablespoons calamus or orris root with strawberry oil
2 measures strawberry leaves	
1 measure dark pink globe amaranth flowers	½ tablespoon calamus or orris root with bergamot oil
½ measure dried mint leaves and/or flowers	½ tablespoon calamus or orris root with mint oil

Prepare the oil and fixative mixtures in advance, then mix all the ingredients together and store in large screw-top jars in a dark place. Shake them regularly during this time. Display with silica dried pink roses.

LAVENDER SACHETS
FOR THE LINEN CUPBOARD

When you are making up pot-pourri for sachets, the mixture will be invisible, so there is no point in wasting beautiful roses and other perfect flowers on it: use up all your broken pieces instead. It is also important to choose a long-lasting fragrance for the sachet so that it doesn't have to be renewed too often.

I find the most efficient way of filling sachets is to use a much higher proportion of fixative, powdered this time, so that the bulk of the sachet is kept to a minimum but the strength of the fragrance is reliable. If you are only making a few sachets then you need only use a powdered fixative and oil mixture, but if you are planning to make quite a few sachets it will be cheaper to pad out the mixture with some dried lavender and other small items. A final possibility is to use up leftover amounts of bulky pot-pourri, put them in a strong polythene bag (check it doesn't have any holes in it) and crush the contents with a rolling pin. You could use a blender instead but it is likely to retain the flavour of the pot-pourri no

matter how thoroughly you wash it out, so the rolling pin method is best unless you want to devote your blender to this task.

LAVENDER, SWEET LAVENDER

4 measures lavender flowers	1 tablespoon powdered calamus or orris root with rose oil
1 measure rose petals	
2 tablespoons powdered calamus or orris root with lavender oil	1 tablespoon powdered calamus or orris root with allspice oil

Mix the ingredients together and allow to mature in screw-topped jars for about 2-3 weeks. The mixture can then be used to fill small lacy sachets for use in drawers or linen cupboards.

MOTH BOMBS

2 measures lavender flowers	2 tablespoons powdered calamus or orris root with lavender oil
2 measures cloves	
2 tablespoons powdered calamus or orris root with clove oil	

Mix the ingredients together and leave in a screw-top jar for a couple of weeks to mature. Then take some lace-edged handkerchiefs and place a heap of the mixture in the centre of each one. Draw up the sides and secure tightly with a small elastic band. Tie a length of satin ribbon around the elastic band and into a loop to hang up the sachet. These sachets can be hung in wardrobes or anywhere else that moths may lurk!

THERE IS SOMETHING WONDERFULLY OLD-FASHIONED AND COMFORTING ABOUT PLACING LAVENDER BAGS IN DRAWERS AND CUPBOARDS, AND THEY CERTAINLY GIVE YOUR CLOTHES AND LINEN A DELICIOUS SMELL.

SCENTED SACHETS FOR
DRAWERS AND CUPBOARDS

Tucking small sachets into drawers of clothes or papers is a lovely, romantic idea. Whenever you open the drawer the fragrance wafts up at you and leaves a delicious lingering scent on everything kept in the drawer. Again, I use a powdered fixative for these sachets as it is less bulky, but you could use a standard bulky pot-pourri and crush it to fill a sachet if you prefer.

Sachets are simple to make, either by hand or machine. You merely cut out two pieces of fabric the same size and, placing them right sides together, sew around three sides. Turn the bag the right way out and fill with the pot-pourri. Sew along the fourth side to close and trim with lace or ribbons, depending on your taste. I must confess to using lace-edged handkerchiefs a great deal; I find it much easier to make little bundles tied with ribbon, as described in the Moth Bomb recipe, than to make rectangular sachets.

The choice of fragrance is completely up to you. I have included some of my own recipes here but by all means substitute your own ingredients if you prefer. Make a good selection of powdered calamus or orris root and oil mixtures and store them in clearly labelled jars at least two days before you want to start work.

THESE HERBAL DRAWER SACHETS ARE LOVELY PRESENTS, SO MAKE DOUBLE THE AMOUNT OF YOUR CHOSEN MIXTURE AND THEN YOU CAN KEEP SOME WHILE STILL HAVING PLENTY TO GIVE AWAY!

VICTORIAN ROSE

1 measure rose petals	1 tablespoon powdered calamus or orris root with patchouli oil
2 tablespoons powdered calamus or orris root with rose oil	1 tablespoon powdered calamus or orris root with allspice oil

Mix all the ingredients together and leave in a screw-topped jar for a couple of weeks, shaking regularly. Use to fill sachets and bags.

GARDEN BOUQUET

3 measures rose petals	2 tablespoons powdered calamus or orris root with carnation oil
2 measures lavender flowers	
3 tablespoons powdered calamus or orris root with rose oil	1 tablespoon powdered calamus or orris root with clove oil
2 tablespoons powdered calamus or orris root with lavender oil	1 tablespoon powdered calamus or orris root with cinnamon oil

Mix all the ingredients together and store in a screw-topped jar for a couple of weeks, shaking regularly. The pot-pourri mixture is then ready to fill sachets and bags.

SIMMERING POT-POURRI
This pot-pourri is particularly suitable for Christmas and other celebratory times when you want the house to smell especially delicious. I use it to cheer us up on a gloomy day, because it's really uplifting to have the soft scent of fresh peaches or summer flowers wafting through the house. Now that oils are available in such scents as chocolate and vanilla, you could also cheer up a chocaholic by making some chocolate and mint simmering pot-pourri and gently simmering it in the kitchen. On the other hand, maybe it wouldn't cheer them up and they would consider it gentle torture.

There are several ways to use these mixtures. You can simmer them in water in a small old saucepan on top of the cooker. They can be laid dry on a baking tray (don't use it for cakes afterwards!) which is placed in a cool oven with the door left open. Finally, you can buy a special steamer which consists of a small bowl on a stand with a small night light underneath it. I believe in America you can also buy electric versions of this steamer, but I have not yet seen one for sale in Britain. I own several of these small steamers so that I can make a particular room in the house smell fresh or flowery. (For details of where to buy these steamers see the list of suppliers at the back of the book.)

These recipes are even more simple than those for ordinary pot-pourri because you do not need to mature the mixture before using it. Here are some examples that you could copy or improve upon according to your taste.

WASSAIL BOWL

1 measure chopped dried apple slices	1 tablespoon cut calamus or orris root with sweet orange oil
1 measure broken cinnamon sticks	
1 measure dried and chopped orange peel	1 tablespoon cut calamus or orris root with apple oil
1 measure allspice berries	1 tablespoon cut calamus or orris root with allspice oil
1 measure cloves	

Mix the oils and fixatives in the usual way, then mix all the other ingredients together. Keep in a screw-topped storage jar. To use this recipe, I put half a measure of it, with a little water, into an old saucepan and simmer it as gently as possible. If you are using it on a baking tray there is no need to add water. If using the small steamers then you will need to use less than half a measure, according to the exact size of the steamer.

SUMMER FLOWERS

1 measure rose petals	1 tablespoon cut calamus or orris root with jasmin oil
1 measure cornflowers	
1 measure jasmin flowers	1 tablespoon cut calamus or orris root with carnation oil
1 tablespoon cut calamus or orris root with rose oil	

Mix all the ingredients and store in a screw-topped jar. Simmer following your preferred method.

SPRING FLOWERS

1 measure violet leaves	1 tablespoon cut calamus or orris root with neroli oil
1 measure narcissi flowers	
1 measure rose petals	1 tablespoon cut calamus or orris root with rose geranium oil
1 measure rose leaves	
2 tablespoons cut calamus or orris root with violet oil	

Mix all the ingredients and store in a screw-topped jar. Simmer following your preferred method.

SIMMERING POT-POURRI IS AN EXCELLENT WAY TO FILL THE HOUSE WITH A WELCOMING SCENT, SO THIS WASSAIL BOWL MIX (see page 99) WOULD BE ESPECIALLY APPROPRIATE FOR GREETING GUESTS AT CHRISTMAS-TIME.

You can use the mixture more than once, but it is important to strain and dry it out between uses otherwise it will develop a life of its own and turn furry.

SLEIGH BELLS IN THE SNOW

1 measure pine needles	1 tablespoon cut calamus or orris root with rose oil
1 measure orange peel	
1 measure hawthorn berries	1 tablespoon cut calamus or orris root with cinnamon oil
1 measure mistletoe leaves	
1 tablespoon cut calamus or orris root with pine oil	1 tablespoon cut calamus or orris root with clove oil

Mix all the ingredients and store in a screw-topped jar. Simmer following your preferred method.

AUTUMN WOODS

1 measure pine needles	1 tablespoon cut calamus or orris root with sandalwood oil
1 measure tiny pine cones	
1 measure chopped autumn leaves	1 tablespoon cut calamus or orris root with orange oil
1 tablespoon cut calamus or orris root with pine oil	1 tablespoon cut calamus or orris root with allspice oil

Mix all the ingredients and store in a screw-topped jar. Simmer following your preferred method.

BATH-TIME BUBBLES

Relaxing in a warm, delightfully fragrant bath must be one of the best ways to start or finish the day. Showers are refreshing and can be invigorating but I'm not convinced that they have the same unwinding effects as a warm, unhurried bath. There are many products on the market for use in the bath and shower, but it is great fun to experiment with some home-made alternatives which, because they are made from completely natural herbs and oils, must be better for your skin.

Bathrooms also look good when sporting collections of pretty perfume bottles and soaps on a shelf or display area. Visiting your bathroom is an extra treat for guests if you put out some unusual homemade bath potions that they can try; the only problem is the length of time they stay in the bathroom!

ORANGE BLOSSOM DREAMS

This oil smells wonderful, costs very little to make, makes you feel deliciously relaxed and is good for your skin – what more could you ask?

150 ml (5 fl oz) sweet almond oil	2 teaspoons (10 ml) sweet orange essential oil
2 tablespoons (30 ml) neroli (orange blossom) essential oil	

Mix all the oils together and pour them into a bottle that is large enough to allow you to shake the mixture well. Give it its first good shake, then put in a warm place for a week or so, shaking it whenever you remember. To use it, pour some into a drawn bath and stir it around really well.

HERBAL TRANQUILITY

150 ml (5 fl oz) sweet almond oil	1 teaspoon (5 ml) sage essential oil
3 teaspoons (15 ml) mint essential oil	2 teaspoons (10 ml) bergamot essential oil
1 teaspoon (5 ml) lemon verbena essential oil	1 teaspoon (5 ml) rosemary essential oil

Mix all the oils together and pour into a generously sized bottle. Shake well, then leave in a warm place for a week and shake at frequent intervals. Pour into a drawn bath and mix well.

LITTLE MUSLIN BAGS FILLED WITH FRESH HERBS OR AROMATIC FLOWERS, SUCH AS ORANGE BLOSSOM, ARE QUICK TO MAKE. THEY ARE SUSPENDED FROM THE BATH TAPS SO THE HOT WATER CAN RUN OVER THEM AND RELEASE THEIR FRAGRANCE. IF YOU WANT TO GIVE AWAY YOUR OWN BATH ESSENCES AS PRESENTS, HUNT OUT ATTRACTIVE BOTTLES FOR THEM AND SUCCESS WILL BE ENSURED!

STRAWBERRY SUMMER

150 ml (5 fl oz) sweet almond oil	2 teaspoons (10 ml) sweet orange essential oil
2 tablespoons (30 ml) strawberry essential oil	

Mix all the oils together and pour them into a generously sized bottle. Shake well, then leave in a warm place for a week and shake at frequent intervals. Pour into a drawn bath and mix well.

TRADITIONAL FLOWERS

150 ml (5 fl oz) sweet almond oil	1 teaspoon (5 ml) clove essential oil
1 tablespoon (15 ml) lavender essential oil	1 teaspoon (5 ml) carnation essential oil
1 tablespoon (15 ml) rose essential oil	

Mix all the oils together and pour into a generously sized bottle. Shake well, then leave in a warm place for a week and shake at frequent intervals. Pour into a drawn bath and mix well.

HAND-MADE VALENTINES AND BIRTHDAY CARDS

Cards that have been hand-made always carry much more meaning and give far more pleasure than commercially made ones. No matter how high or low your standard of artistic ability, there is always something you can make yourself to send as a greeting or thought to a family member or friend.

Dried and pressed flowers are particularly easy to incorporate into a card. Pressed flowers can be attached to the card with a latex adhesive, but they must always be covered with a thin clear plastic film, otherwise they can easily become damaged or torn. Dried flowers should be attached to the card with glue, and I prefer to use a hot-glue gun because it's quick, easy and neat. If, however, you feel rather nervous about experimenting with a hot-glue gun you could use another type of glue, but should allow time for the glue to dry.

Many shapes can be cut from plain or patterned papers, such as hearts or Christmas trees. A group of Christmas trees cut from different shades of green origami paper look very attractive, or a selection of hearts in various shades of pink could look effective for Valentine's Day. Simple paper folding is another possibility. Small rectangles of paper pleated into fan, in co-ordinating colours, look lovely and only take a few moments to create.

If you have a leftover piece of wrapping paper that is particularly pretty, you could cover the front of a blank card with it, holding it in place with double-sided tape around the edges. This gives the effect of a parcel which you can then decorate with ribbons and a miniature gift tag.

I always treasure home-made cards, as no doubt most people do, and have quite a collection of beautifully embroidered Christmas and birthday cards sent by friends from all over the world. If you are keen on sewing, there are many lovely kits available for making small designs for cards, but with time being at such a premium in my life at the moment I have to resort to quicker methods for home-made cards than that!

When I was in America recently, I found some beautiful cards that were made by sticking spices and seed heads in patterns on to cream card backgrounds. There were some really intricate patterns and swirls which looked very effective. It's easy to amass a collection of the smaller seeds by looking at the spice selection in your local supermarket. Mustard seeds, poppy seeds, coriander and cardamom, peppercorns in various colours, caraway and salt crystals are just a few possibilities. I have now experimented with some, and found latex adhesive the easiest glue to use. If you squeeze a small amount into a saucer, you can dip the seeds gently into the glue (holding them with a fine pair of tweezers) before arranging them on the card. Do not use too much glue otherwise it will detract from your design. Larger spices can be used, such as cinnamon sticks, ginger root, liquorice roots, nuts or even small cones. Once you start a collection of pretty bits and pieces, such as beads, lace and ribbons, ideas for using them will gradually come to you as you play around with the various ingredients.

GIFT-WRAPPING

Wrapping presents is something that you either love or hate. I really enjoy wrapping presents, if I have the time to think up some unusual ideas. Sadly, however, time is usually running out and at three o'clock on Christmas morning I'm far more worried about getting everything wrapped before the household starts waking up than devising unusual wrapping ideas. Oh well, maybe next year . . .

Getting organized

Organization is probably the best way to make gift-wrapping easier. Large rolls of florists' ribbon are moderately inexpensive and go a very long way. I have several rolls of these ribbons, in co-ordinating colours, which are hung on a towel rail in my work room. That way, it's easy to see which colour is best, to pull off as much as you want and also to find the rolls of ribbon when you need them. At Christmas, when there is so much wrapping to be done, it makes most sense to choose a particular colour scheme for your gift-wrapping and buy a large quantity of suitable wrapping paper in one or two designs, plus plenty of ribbon in perhaps two co-ordinating colours. You will then have enough paper and ribbon for the larger parcels and the smaller parcels can be wrapped in the off-cuts. Wrap the largest parcels first, and then you will be able to see how much paper you have left. If you

often leave wrapping presents until the very last minute, then do make sure you have good stocks of a plain but attractive paper that can be used all year round, to make absolutely sure you don't run out of paper after the shops have shut on Christmas Eve!

Wrapping huge presents

One of the real problems of gift-wrapping is the giant-sized present. Maybe it is a useful wheelbarrow or a great big teddy bear, but either present will be hard to wrap. The solution I have used for several years now comes in the form of very large black plastic dustbin bags. These sacks are very cheap to buy and the item either can be loosely wrapped with tissue paper first if it has any sharp corners or just put straight into the sack. Tie up the sack with twine or a strong elastic band to make sure it is secure. You can then go to town with ribbon or tinsel decorations. If you use inexpensive florist's ribbon to tie a lavish bow with lots of streamers and add a giant gift tag (either make one yourself or use a full-size card), you have a very eye-catching parcel.

GIVEN THE CHOICE BETWEEN A HAND-MADE CARD AND ONE BOUGHT FROM A SHOP, I KNOW WHICH ONE I'D PREFER. IF YOU'VE NEVER MADE YOUR OWN CARDS BEFORE, IT'S A GOOD IDEA TO PRACTISE BEFORE USING YOUR MOST PRIZED FLOWERS AND CARDS.

Material effects

Another point to bear in mind when you are thinking about wrapping a present is that some fabrics can actually work out a lot cheaper than wrapping paper. Remnants of pretty floral fabric or a crisp gingham or tartan look great as a wrapping medium and can work out at half the price of attractive high-quality wrapping paper. Other fabrics I often use are net and tulle. If you are wrapping something vaguely spherical, then cut out large circles of net and lay them one over the other. Place the gift in the centre and gather up the edges of the net around it and secure with wire or an elastic band. Then tie lots of ribbons and frills around the wire or elastic band and you have a large *bonbonière*-style gift.

Bags of style

Perhaps the easiest way of all to wrap presents that have a slightly awkward shape is to buy a selection of attractive carrier bags that are sold specifically for gift-wrapping. Add some sheets of tissue paper, some shredded tissue paper and a selection of pretty ribbons in appropriate colours, and most of your wrapping problems are over. Wrap your gift in the tissue paper and then place it inside the bag. Cover with shredded tissue paper until it starts spilling over the top of the bag, then tie the handles together with a couple of ribbons in complementary colours for an expensive-looking result.

One example I often make up for my courses uses a carrier bag with black polka dots on a white background. The gift is wrapped in black tissue paper, placed in the bag and then covered with heaps of shredded black tissue. The handles are then tied together with a black and white tartan ribbon, a string of pearls and a black velvet ribbon. Incidentally, the pearls are bought by the roll from a specialist supplier; I didn't mean a wearable string of pearls, although come to think of it I'd love a present tied up like that. How glamorous!

Ribbons and bows

These play a very important role in gift-wrapping and it is worth looking around for unusual styles and colours. I have an old box which I use for storing useful bits of ribbon – in some cases they are far too nice to use so they are taken out and then put back again. My favourite type of ribbon is the kind with narrow wires threaded down each side, which make it wonderfully easy to tie pretty bows and keep them in the right shape.

Collect some inexpensive ribbons and also a few really special pieces and then, when you come to wrap up a parcel, you can decide whether you can face parting with your more treasured pieces. Generally, I would say that cheaper ribbons and paper florists' ribbon are the most useful, bearing in mind that there is a limit to the amount you probably want to spend on the wrappings. Even so, there may be times when you want to splash out on some marvellously wide and expensive velvet or satin ribbons, and really make your gift look special.

To tie a good bow, it may be easiest to make a figure of eight and then to wire it (see diagram). Alternatively, if you have

THIS DIAGRAM SHOWS HOW TO WIRE A PIECE OF RIBBON INTO A SECURE BOW.

very nimble fingers and find it easy to tie bows, you can use the traditional method instead. Another option is to make a heap of curls by running the bevelled edge of a pair of scissors along the length of a piece of curling ribbon (most paper ribbon sold in florists and gift shops will do this).

Bought paper ribbon bows are a fairly expensive way of decorating a parcel and these bows can be made at home for much less money. If you refer to the diagram, it is fairly simple. Just make four equal-sized loops with florists' ribbon, then make four slightly smaller loops and finally one small loop to fit in the middle. I use a double-sided tape to secure the ends of the loops together, but you won't need to use tape at all if your ribbon is the type that sticks to itself when moistened.

Gift themes

Thinking up a theme for gift-wrapping can be fun. If you are giving something to a gardener, you could wrap the gift in hessian, tie it with lots of green garden twine and make a gift tag like a seed packet. A father's day present could be wrapped in pages from a fishing newspaper or magazine, tied in fishing line and decorated with a fish-shaped gift tag and some fishing flies. If he is a keen football fan then you could use pages from a football magazine, tie the parcel with a small version of a football scarf and make a football-shaped gift tag.

The more you think, the more variations will spring to mind. For a young ballet fan, the present could be wrapped in many layers of pink net, tied with satin ballet shoe ribbons and decorated with a gift tag shaped like a pair of ballet shoes. For a horse enthusiast, how about wrapping the parcel in tissue paper and then burying it under some hay in a home-made hessian nose-bag. I'm sure that once you start thinking along these lines, depending upon the particular interest of the recipient of your gift, ideas will start to blossom.

As a final suggestion, keep your eyes open for unusual containers. I have wrapped a present very effectively in a large terra-cotta flower pot. Old (or new) baskets can make a gift look even better, pretty tins, boxes and other treasures can be found by looking around local antique and junk shops and may well cost less than you imagine. The main gift that people appreciate the most is the time, trouble and thought that you have put into their presents, to make them extra special.

EDIBLE GIFTS

Everyone loves receiving extra special home-made goodies as presents, and sweets, pickles and chutneys, jams and jellies are always popular gifts to receive.

Packaging is of paramount importance; if you tip some dog-eared peppermint creams into an old tea caddy, still containing some leftover tea leaves, they will look far less appetizing than if they had been put in a pretty box with fancy wrapping. The big exception to this applies to anyone under ten (hence my accurate description of the packaging). When you are presented with some lovingly made peppermint creams, no matter how odd-looking, by a daughter who is obviously very proud of her efforts, then it doesn't matter whether they are packed in gold leaf *petits four* cases or an old tea tin. It's the thought that counts.

Making cookies or pickles are good starting points for younger children. Obviously they will need careful supervision, as even the most confident children can burn themselves on a hot oven (I seem to manage it often enough), but if they can succeed in making something for Daddy, Grandma or any other lucky relative, that will give them much more pleasure than if you provide the money, or even the present.

Pretty packaging

There are many attractive tins and boxes available nowadays, and these can be very useful for packaging the goodies you make. Attractive glass bottles filled with a selection of herbal and spicy oils or vinegars would make a lovely gift for an enthusiastic cook. If you keep your eyes open when out shopping you will be amazed at how many standard supermarket products are actually packaged in very prettily shaped bottles, jars and containers. Most speciality vinegars come in elegant tall bottles, and if you change the screw top for a cork and wrap a gingham or plain ribbon around it you have a most attractive container.

THESE SPICY ALMONDS MAKE DELICIOUS GIFTS BUT THEY ARE ALSO IDEAL FOR SERVING WITH DRINKS BEFORE A DINNER PARTY, SO YOU MAY WANT TO KEEP SOME FOR YOURSELF!

Labels

Labelling is also very important when giving things you have made at home. Details of the ingredients may be excessive, but do say how long the present will keep and whether or not to refrigerate it. If you are making something a little out of the ordinary then a serving suggestion or some recipes that include that delicacy would be very useful. These could be tied around the neck of the bottle with narrow ribbon and will add to the presentation.

Whatever you choose to make for a friend or member of the family, you can be sure that it will be remembered long after the run of the mill gifts, such as talcum powder and hand cream, have been forgotten. I expect you're thinking that there is no time to make all these ideas, but we all find time for the things we really want to do, so perhaps making our own presents should come a little higher on our lists?

BOURBON NUTS

These nuts are simply delicious and make useful presents for fathers and uncles, for whom it is often hard to find something. A selection of cocktail nibbles would be fun, perhaps with the ingredients for a cocktail?

225 g (8 oz) demerara sugar	450 g (1 lb) whole mixed nuts
175 ml (6 fl oz) Bourbon whiskey	50 g (2 oz) butter
	water

MAKES ABOUT 450 G (1 LB)

Put the Bourbon and sugar in a pan and bring to the boil. Boil for 3 minutes. Remove from the heat and add the mixed nuts, stirring really well until the sugar turns white and grainy. Return the saucepan to the heat, add a few drops of water and melt the sugar again. Watching carefully that the sugar does not burn, cook for about 2 minutes or until the syrup has turned a caramel colour. Remove from the heat and stir in the butter.

Turn the nuts out of the saucepan on to a really well greased baking sheet and spread them out so each one is separate. Leave to cool. These nuts can be kept in an airtight container for up to 2 weeks.

SPICY ALMONDS

This is another useful nut recipe. Perhaps you could make these and the Bourbon Nuts, and package them in a two-compartment dish with a cellophane covering and pretty bow.

450 g (1 lb) whole blanched almonds	10 g (2 tsp) medium hot curry powder
50 g (2 oz) unsalted butter	5 g (1 tsp) garam masala
	pinch of sugar
5 g (1 tsp) sea salt	

————— MAKES ABOUT 450 G (1 LB) —————

Melt the butter in a frying pan and add the almonds, tossing and stirring them well until they are a light golden brown. Add the other ingredients and continue cooking and stirring well for another couple of minutes. Drain the nuts on sheets of kitchen roll and leave to cool. These nuts will keep for a week in an airtight container.

ALMOND AND COCONUT COOKIES

I'm particularly keen on coconut, but chocolate seems to be more popular with the rest of the family.

60 g (2½ oz) shredded coconut	1 large egg
50 g (2 oz) flaked almonds	5 ml (1 tsp) vanilla essence
90 g (3½ oz) rolled oats	250 g (9 oz) demerara sugar
100 g (4 oz) butter	

————— MAKES ABOUT 30 —————

Cream the sugar and butter together until light and creamy. Add the egg and vanilla essence and beat really well. Stir in all the remaining ingredients. Using a teaspoon, pile spoonfuls of the mixture on to a greased baking tray. Allow at least 2.5-4 cm (1-1½ in) between each pile to allow the cookies to spread. Bake in a pre-heated oven at 180°C (350°F), Gas Mark 4 for about 10 minutes. Do not allow the cookies to darken too much. Leave to cool on a wire rack.

PEANUT BUTTER, CHOCOLATE CHIP AND PEANUT COOKIES

This is another recipe that would not win prizes in the battle against tooth decay but nevertheless tastes delicious. A little of what you fancy does you good, maybe?

150 g (5 oz) shelled peanuts	175 g (6 oz) smooth peanut butter
150 g (5 oz) chocolate chips	2 large eggs
175 g (6 oz) rolled oats	100 ml (4 fl oz) milk
250 g (9 oz) demerara sugar	300 g (11 oz) flour
	pinch of salt
250 g (9 oz) granulated sugar	5 ml (1 tsp) vanilla essence
175 g (6 oz) butter	5 g (1 tsp) baking powder

————— MAKES ABOUT 40 —————

Cream together the peanut butter, butter, brown and white sugars, vanilla essence and salt. Beat really well until light and creamy. Add the eggs one at a time and beat again really well. Sift in the baking powder and flour, then add the milk. Stir well until all the ingredients are well incorporated, then add the oats, peanuts and chocolate chips. Using a teaspoon drop spoonfuls on to a well greased baking tray, leaving about 2.5-5 cm (1-2 in) between each heap for the cookies to spread. Bake in a pre-heated oven at 180°C (350°F), Gas Mark 4 for 10 minutes. Take out of the oven and, once they have cooled slightly, place on a wire rack.

DOUBLE CHOC CHIP COOKIES

Here is another recipe that works well, but the finished cookies have to be hidden from adults and children alike if any are to survive 'testing' long enough to be given as presents!

200 g (7 oz) good-quality plain chocolate	50 g (2 oz) castor sugar
	1 large egg
225 g (8 oz) self-raising flour	100 g (4 oz) chocolate chips
200 g (7 oz) butter	1 tsp (15 ml) vanilla essence
75 g (3 oz) demerara sugar	

— MAKES ABOUT 30 —

Melt the chocolate in a bowl over a pan of hot water. Mix together the two sugars, butter and vanilla essence in a bowl and, using an electric whisk, beat until light and fluffy. Add the egg and beat again. Then gently stir in the sifted flour and melted chocolate, add the chocolate chips and refrigerate for about 1 hour.

When the dough is chilled, make it into 2.5 cm (1 in) balls, either with a spoon or clean hands, and place them at least 5 cm (2 in) apart on a greased baking sheet. Bake in a pre-heated oven at 190°C (375°F), Gas Mark 5 for about 10-15 minutes. Allow to cool slightly and then carefully transfer to a wire rack. These cookies can be frozen or will keep in an airtight container for up to a week.

CHRISTMAS TREE COOKIES

These are very similar to the cornflake and chocolate mixtures that are known and loved by everyone. They are very popular cookies to make but I can't guarantee that there would be anything left to give after a session of making these with the children. Perhaps you should plan on making them by yourself one evening if you want to make sure they don't all get eaten.

200 g (7 oz) white marshmallows	150 g (5 oz) Coco Pops cereal
100 g (4 oz) butter	vegetable oil
5 ml (1 tsp) brown food colouring	

FEW PEOPLE CAN RESIST HOME-MADE COOKIES, AND A LAVISHLY DECORATED BISCUIT TIN CONTAINING AN ASSORTMENT OF THEM WOULD BE A MARVELLOUS GIFT FOR A FAMILY.

Melt the butter and marshmallows over a low heat. Cook gently for about 5 minutes, stirring all the time. Take the pan off the heat and add the food colouring, whisking until it is well incorporated. Stir in the Coco Pops and cover evenly with the marshmallow mixture. Keep the mixture warm, but not cooking, by placing the saucepan in a very large mixing bowl filled with very hot water. Do not let the water come in contact with the marshmallow mixture.

Lightly oil your fingers, then take 1 tbsp (15 g) of the mixture and place it on a sheet of greaseproof paper. Carefully mould the mixture into a small wreath shape and place on a greased baking tray. Repeat this until all the mixture has been used, then leave in a cool place until the mixture has set firm.

Once the wreaths have set they can be decorated with silver and gold balls, or piped with icing. As well as being edible, they also make lovely little Christmas tree ornaments if they are tied on with narrow gold string or crochet cotton.

For a different effect, you can use green food colouring and plain Rice Crispies, or any other cereal.

CHRISTMAS TREE BISCUITS

These are lovely classic-looking Christmas biscuits. Once they are cool the children can help to decorate them; they don't disappear as quickly as the Christmas Tree Cookies.

175 g (6 oz) butter	pinch of salt
150 g (5 oz) sugar	zest of 1 orange
300 g (11 oz) self-raising flour	1 large egg

Cream the butter and sugar together until light and fluffy, then add the egg and zest of the orange. Beat really well until all ingredients are thoroughly combined. Sieve in the salt and flour and fold in gently. Gather the dough into a ball and flatten it

THE CHRISTMAS TREE DOESN'T ONLY HAVE TO BE DECORATED WITH BAUBLES AND CANDLES – YOU CAN USE EDIBLE DECORATIONS AS WELL. BOTH THE CHRISTMAS TREE COOKIES (ABOVE) AND THE CHRISTMAS TREE BISCUITS (LEFT) LOOK GOOD HANGING FROM THE TREE, BUT THEY ARE ALSO LOVELY TO EAT WITH TEA OR COFFEE.

slightly, wrap in greaseproof paper or cling-film and chill in the refrigerator for an hour.

Using a lightly floured board and rolling pin, roll out the pastry until it is between 3-6 mm (⅛-¼ in) thick. Then, using a tree-shaped biscuit cutter, cut out as many Christmas trees as you can. (If you cannot buy a suitably shaped cutter, you can make a cardboard template and cut around that.) Gather up all the scraps and reroll them to avoid wasting any of the mixture. Place them on a greased and floured baking tray.

Bake in a pre-heated oven at 180°C (350°F), Gas Mark 4 for about 10 minutes until the cookies are a light golden colour. Remove them from the tray and place on a wire rack. Before they cool, pierce a hole about 18 mm (¾ in) from the top of each biscuit, using a skewer or knitting needle, so you can thread them with ribbon if you wish to hang them from the tree. Once they are cold, the biscuits can be piped with royal icing, painted with edible food colourings or decorated with silver and gold balls glued on with dabs of royal icing. These biscuits keep well in an airtight tin.

MINIATURE CHRISTMAS CAKES

These are delightful gifts that you can easily personalize. Use the following recipe but bake in very small tins, according to the size of cake you want to give. If you want to make a square cake, then use a rectangular tin and cut the cooked cake into several squares.

225 g (8 oz) plain flour	150 ml (¼ pint) brandy or Calvados
225 g (8 oz) dark brown sugar	4 large eggs
225 g (8 oz) butter	5 g (1 tsp) ground nutmeg
275 g (10 oz) currants	
275 g (10 oz) sultanas	5 g (1 tsp) mixed spice
100 g (4 oz) raisins	pinch of mace
100 g (4 oz) stem ginger in syrup	pinch of salt
175 g (6 oz) dried apricots	zest and juice of one lemon
75 g (3 oz) ground almonds	

━━━ MAKES A 20 CM (8 IN) CAKE ━━━

A MINIATURE CHRISTMAS CAKE IS AN IDEAL GIFT FOR SOMEONE WHO LIVES ON THEIR OWN AND WOULDN'T BOTHER TO MAKE A CAKE JUST FOR THEMSELVES. YOU CAN DECORATE IT IN ALL SORTS OF WAYS, ACCORDING TO THE TASTE OF THE RECIPIENT.

Prepare all the fruit the day before you want to make the cake. Chop the apricots and ginger, then place all the fruit, including the zest and juice of the lemon, in a bowl and pour over the brandy or Calvados. Stir from time to time as you pass during the day. Cover and leave overnight.

Line a 20 cm (8 in) cake tin with a double layer of buttered greaseproof paper. Beat the butter and sugar together in a bowl until creamy and light in colour. Add the eggs, beating thoroughly. Stir in the ground almonds and then carefully fold in the sifted flour, spices and salt. Finally, add the fruit and mix well together.

Pour the mixture into the tin and bake in a pre-heated oven at 140°C (275°F), Gas Mark 1 for 3½-4 hours. A time-honoured tip that I don't always follow is to put 600 ml (1 pint) of water in a meat roasting tin and place it at the bottom of the oven to create the humidi... ...s to produce ...ial perhaps if ...r cake than ...tant for one

...ve it to cool ...n wrap it in ...leave in a ...Perhaps I ...e! ...ith marzi- ...each cake ...e brandy. ...er the top ...e excess ...Roll out ... deeper ...ake and ...e seam

There are many ways to decorate the cakes: here are just two ideas to get your mind working overtime! Think of a theme that will please the recipient or just do something pretty that couldn't fail to please whoever you gave it to.

SNOW SCENE

A classic Christmas cake decoration is to cover the marzipan with royal icing (see below) and to swirl it with a fork to give a rough, snowy effect. Then add some novelties on the top, such as a robin, tree or whatever else you may come across, and tie some ribbon around the sides of the cake.

ROYAL ICING

Place 3 large egg whites in a large clean mixing bowl and sift in 450 g (1 lb) icing sugar. Using an electric whisk, beat on a slow speed until most of the icing sugar is incorporated into the egg whites. Increase the speed to high and continue for about 5 minutes until the mixture is glossy and forms peaks when you remove the whisk.

TEDDY WITH PRESENTS

This idea is probably more suitable for children than adults, unless you are making it for a childish adult like me! I would love to receive a little teddy like this as a home-made Christmas present.

Cover the marzipanned cake with rolled out sugarpaste or fondant icing in whichever colour you want. Then colour a little marzipan dark or light brown depending on the type of bear you want to create! Make a roughly pear-shaped body and a head, then make two small round ears which are attached to the head with beaten egg white. Make two arms and attach those with egg white as well. Add the finishing touches by piping on some white and brown royal icing to make the eyes, nose and mouth, or use small pieces of marzipan or sugarpaste.

Then, make some presents from cubes of either marzipan or sugarpaste, and paint them with edible food colourings. Attach them all to the cake with a little piped royal icing. If you wish, the parcels can be tied with narrow ribbons or cord to give a more realistic effect. You can also tie a ribbon around the cake if you want to add that final festive touch.

MINIATURE CHRISTMAS PUDDINGS

First follow the recipe for the large Christmas pudding (see page 79–80) or follow the alternative recipe given here. The little puddings are made by modelling portions of the large pudding mixture and covering them with melted chocolate.

100 g (4 oz) dried apricots	3 large eggs
100 g (4 oz) dried figs	250 g (9 oz) brown sugar
150 g (5 oz) dates	300 ml (½ pint) double cream
200 g (7 oz) sultanas	400 g (14 oz) plain flour
150 g (5 oz) seedless raisins	5 g (1 tsp) nutmeg
100 g (4 oz) candied peel	5 g (1 tsp) bicarbonate of soda
100 g (4 oz) currants	500 g (18 oz) good-quality plain chocolate
100 g (4 oz) preserved stem ginger	brandy or other liqueurs

Chop the fruits fairly small. Beat together in a large mixing bowl the eggs and brown sugar until they are thick and creamy. Add all the fruit and the double cream. Mix well, then sieve the flour, nutmeg and bicarbonate of soda into the mixture. Make sure all the ingredients are well incorporated, then turn into greased pudding basins. Cover with greaseproof paper and aluminium foil, or a piece of muslin, and steam for about 5 hours. Do not let the puddings boil dry.

Once the pudding is cold, take large tea-spoonfuls of the mixture and, making sure your hands are very clean, roll it into small balls. Melt the chocolate in a basin over a pan of hot water and dip the pudding balls into the chocolate. Stand them on a plate covered with greaseproof paper or aluminium foil and refrigerate until set.

When the chocolate has set, take a small syringe and inject a little brandy or liqueur into the puddings. It is best to stick the syringe in the bottom of each pudding so that the hole does not show. Then place the puddings in *petits four* cases and keep refrigerated until needed.

MARZIPAN APPLES

These pretty little fruits can be packaged in tiny baskets or birds' nests, and I have even presented them in miniature hat boxes which I have made myself.

225 g (8 oz) block of white marzipan	cloves
yellow food colouring	pink blush food colouring powder
green food colouring	

Knead a little green and yellow food colouring into a portion of the marzipan until you have a realistic apple green colour. These colourings are usually very strong so you only need add tiny amounts at a time.

Roll a small piece of the coloured marzipan into a ball. Flatten the top and bottom slightly and, using the end of a skewer or crochet needle, make a dent in the bottom of the apple and a hole in the top, with four slight indentations around it. Place the stem of a clove into the apple to resemble a stalk. Then using a fine paintbrush, apply a very small amount of the pink blush powder over some of the apple to give it a rosy tint like a real apple.

Repeat this for the other apples. Alternatively you could fashion some oranges by making orange-coloured marzipan balls and rolling them on the finest side of a grater to give the effect of orange peel. Marzipan strawberries look more realistic if they are given green stems. Ridges and brown shading are important on bananas. I think a bowl filled with all apples or oranges can look very effective, but if you are feeling adventurous then you could try making a mixed bowl of fruit or a small basket with a collection of more exotic fruits such as melons, figs, peaches or grapes.

FACING PAGE: THESE MARZIPAN FRUITS ARE GREAT FUN TO MAKE AND LOOK VERY PRETTY IN AN ATTRACTIVE BOX OR BASKET. THEY ALSO MAKE GOOD *PETITS FOURS* TO SERVE AFTER DINNER.

MINT AND PEAR JELLY

This jelly can be served with many dishes. A selection of several jellies, arranged in a basket with a blue and white tea towel and matching fabric covers to their lids, would make an attractive gift.

FACING PAGE:
A COLLECTION OF
FLAVOURED OILS, HERBAL
VINEGARS AND FRUIT
JELLIES WOULD MAKE A
MARVELLOUS GIFT,
ESPECIALLY IF YOU
PACKED THEM IN AN
ATTRACTIVE BASKET.

5 large sprigs of fresh mint	300 ml (½ pint) cider vinegar
8 tbsp (120 g) finely chopped mint	1.2 litres (2 pints) water
2.3 kg (5 lb) pears, peeled and chopped	sugar

—— MAKES ABOUT 2-2½ KG (6 LB) ——

BELOW: FRESH HERBS
MAKE ALL THE
DIFFERENCE TO THE
TASTE OF FOOD, AND ARE
ESSENTIAL INGREDIENTS
OF THE RECIPES ON THESE
TWO PAGES. MANY OF
THEM ARE EASILY GROWN
IN POTS ON A SUNNY
WINDOW-SILL, SO DON'T
WORRY IF YOU HAVEN'T
GOT A GARDEN.

Put the chopped pears into a pan with the 5 sprigs of mint and cover with the water. Bring to the boil and simmer for about 30 minutes or until the pears are soft and pulpy, stirring occasionally. Add the vinegar and boil for about 5 minutes. Strain the contents of the pan through a jelly bag overnight.

Measure the strained juices and, for every 600 ml (1 pint) of liquid, add 400 g (14 oz) of sugar. Put the juices and sugar into a preserving pan and boil rapidly for about 10 minutes until setting point has been reached. (If you are using a thermometer, setting point is at 221°F [105°C], If not, spoon a little jelly on to a chilled saucer, allow to cool and then push your finger across its surface – it will wrinkle when it has reached setting point.) Skim off any scum that may have formed on the top of the mixture and allow to cool partially. Then add the finely chopped mint and stir well. Have some warm, clean jam jars waiting and pour in the jelly, cover and seal. Label clearly.

CLARET AND CRANBERRY JELLY

Jams and jellies are always useful to keep as standbys, perhaps when you need to give a small gift to say thank you. The colour of this jelly makes it worth standing it on a window-sill just to look pretty.

300 ml (½ pint) claret	900 g (2 lb) cranberries
300 ml (½ pint) water	sugar

—— MAKES 1.4 KG (3 LB) ——

Cover the cranberries with the water in a saucepan or preserving pan. Simmer for about 20-25 minutes or until tender. Strain through a jelly bag overnight.

Measure the strained juice into a pan and add 350 g (12 oz) of sugar for every 600 ml (1 pint) of juice. Cook over a gentle heat, stirring constantly, until the sugar has dissolved. Pour in the claret and bring to the boil. Boil rapidly for about 10 minutes, until setting point is reached. (If you are using a thermometer, setting point is at 221°F [105°C]. If not, spoon a little jelly on to a chilled saucer, allow to cool and then push your finger across its surface – it will wrinkle when it has reached setting point.) Skim any froth off the top and pour into warm, clean jam jars. Cover with waxed paper circles and seal. Label clearly.

BASIL VINEGAR

Keen cooks would be very grateful for some interesting or unusual oils and vinegars. This vinegar is delicious in salad dressings, especially with tomato salads: tomato and basil is a sublime combination.

2.4 litres (4 pints) white wine vinegar	20 sprigs fresh clean basil

MAKES 2.4 LITRES (4 PINTS)

Put the vinegar in a pan and heat to just below boiling point, then leave to cool. Wash and dry the bottles you intend to fill with the vinegar and place about 4 sprigs of fresh basil into each one. Pour in the cooled vinegar and seal the bottles. Stand on a sunny window-sill for a couple of weeks and then put in a darker place for long-term storage.

GINGER AND MINT OIL

This oil adds a lovely tang to stir-fries, salads and sauces. Very little work is needed to make it and it would be an unusual gift.

1.2 litres (2 pints) grapeseed or sunflower oil	2 × 12 mm (½ in) cubes fresh ginger root, sliced
8 sprigs fresh mint, washed and dried	

MAKES 1.2 LITRES (2 PINTS)

Place the ginger root and oil in a pan and heat gently, without boiling, then allow to cool. Wash and dry the bottles you will be using. Place about 3-4 sprigs of mint in each bottle. Discard the ginger root then carefully strain the oil into the bottles and seal them. Leave on a sunny window-sill for a couple of weeks and then strain out the mint leaves. Store in a darker place for long-term storage.

DECORATIONS

First impressions count for a lot, and when guests arrive at your home they will quickly notice whether there are any welcoming decorations around or not. You don't have to spend a huge amount of money or time on making some lovely fresh or dried flower arrangements, and sometimes informal jugs or vases of garden flowers look much more charming and inviting than expensive, rather formal arrangements. In this chapter you will find all sorts of ideas for simple and more complicated decorations that will help to make entertaining a memorable occasion for both you and your guests.

O ne of the most obvious places to decorate, yet frequently ignored, is the front door. This is the first welcoming sign to guests, and if you hang a pretty circle of flowers on the door to greet them, it sets the mood for the occasion before you even answer the door! At Christmas there are many different styles to choose from, but a traditional holly or spruce wreath always looks spectacular.

MAKING WREATHS

I find that the easiest way to make up a wreath with spruce or other evergreen foliage is to use a twig wreath base. These come in various sizes, so decide on the scale of decoration and buy or make one accordingly. Making a twiggy wreath shape is easier than you might think, and lengths of virginia creeper or honeysuckle vine are easy to use. Collect several lengths of flexible stalks that are at least 1.2-1.5 m (4-5 ft) long, then twist them into a circle and tie firmly with wire at several points. If the wreath looks a little under-nourished, add more and more stems until you have the desired effect. Then leave it to dry on a flat surface in a warm place.

THE LOVELY ROUNDED SHAPE AND SUBTLE COLOURING OF POMEGRANATES MAKE THEM IDEAL INGREDIENTS FOR WREATHS, THOUGH I THINK THEY CAN LOOK JUST AS GOOD WHEN DISPLAYED BY THEMSELVES.

Decorating a twig wreath base
Once you have a wreath shape, either bought or home-made, you can think about decorating it. I would recommend using blue spruce, because it keeps its needles very well and looks wonderfully festive. If you cannot get hold of any spruce then use holly, a conifer or any other evergreen shrub instead. Gather together any accessories that you would like to add, such as ribbons, Christmas tree ornaments, fresh or dried flowers, or miniature parcels – the possibilities are endless. I have used dried pomegranates, specially dehydrated bread rolls, gourds, nuts and ribbons on the wreath in the photograph (see pages 116–17) but there are plenty of possibilities to choose from.

You can wire all the decorations in place with medium gauge florists' wire, but I find using a hot-glue gun is much quicker and easier. If you cut the base material into roughly 15 cm (6 in) lengths, you can glue them to the wreath quite easily. Try to avoid the base looking too spare, otherwise it will seem as though you have been mean with your plant material. When you have glued on a liberal covering of your chosen greenery, you can attach wired ribbon bows (see page 104) and the other accessories that you have chosen. If you intend to hang the wreath on the front door and leave it there for any length of time, try to use ingredients that can withstand the prevailing weather conditions.

Decorating a mossy wreath base
Although wreaths are at their most popular in the winter, there is no reason why you cannot welcome guests with a stunning summer wreath as well. Flowers are plentiful during the summer and a wreath made from pretty garden flowers can look even lovelier than the traditional Christmas decoration. It is perfectly possible to make up a summer wreath using the same glue gun technique, which is quick and easy,

DON'T MAKE THE MISTAKE OF THINKING THAT WREATHS ARE FOR WINTER ONLY: THIS SUMMER WREATH, WHICH IS A-FROTH WITH COW PARSLEY, DELPHINIUMS AND STOCKS, WITH A FEW LENGTHS OF TRAILING IVY, HAS PLENTY OF IMPACT AND WOULD BE A WONDERFUL WEDDING DECORATION.

but it does have its drawbacks when dealing with fresh flowers because they will soon fade without water. If you want the wreath to last for a while it would be better to use a mossy base which you can soak with water and which will therefore lengthen the life of the cut flowers that you use.

To make a mossy wreath base you will need some sphagnum moss, which is the type used in hanging baskets and should be available from your local garden centre. You can buy wire wreath shapes from florists and garden centres and you will also need a reel of light gauge florists' wire. Fashion some of the moss into a sausage shape and attach it to the wreath base with the wire. Carry on attaching the moss until all the base is covered and you have a good sturdy base for your decoration. If you are using the hot-glue gun method to make up a wreath then you can use a twiggy wreath base instead.

Try to choose long-lasting components, because the flowers will not receive much moisture even if you are using a moss-covered wreath. Make sure all the flowers have had a good long drink in deep water before you use them in the wreath.

Personally, I prefer to use a twiggy wreath base. I remove the faded flowers and put the base away until I am ready to use it again. I gather the flowers from my garden the previous day and put them in water for a long drink, and then a few hours before the guests arrive I glue the flowers and foliage around the wreath base and add a pretty bow. This way it only takes a few minutes to make the ring, yet it looks fresh and pretty for the evening. The cost is quite low because I grow the flowers myself and can use the same ring over and over again. Even if you have to buy the flowers from a florist, you don't need a great number, provided you use some foliage as well.

GARLANDS

One of the most attractive ways of decorating doorways, fireplaces, cupboards or dressers is to wind a rope of flowers along them. Although a rope or swag of flowers is not as simple to make as a wreath, it looks extremely attractive when finished and with a little determination and practice you should soon be making good headway.

Dried flower ropes

When creating a permanent dried flower decoration you do have the comfort of knowing it will last for many years if looked after properly. A swag of dried flowers has been decorating the dresser in my kitchen for at least three or four years now, and apart from the occasional dust with the hair drier on a low setting it has needed no attention at all. Alternatively you can make a seasonal decoration, perhaps for Christmas, and carefully pack it with tissue paper in a well-sealed box to store in a warm atmosphere whenever it is not needed. Assuming it does not get dropped or damaged in any way, you should be able to hang it up again the following year. Obviously this will depend upon the ingredients, because some dried items last much better than others, but as a general rule you can cover up any bare patches with more dried flowers or foliage and no one will be any the wiser.

When I'm making a dried flower swag I always use a fairly sturdy piece of rope or cord as the base. Bend one end over to make a loop for hanging and wire it firmly, then do the same at the other end and you are ready to begin. Never underestimate how much material you will need to make the rope; it looks far better to make a full chunky rope rather than a long skimpy effort. Measure the length you need, including the curve, by hanging the rope or cord in position. Try to choose a variety of ingredients to give a good overall balance in shape. I often use glycerined leaves because they

THIS DIAGRAM SHOWS HOW A SMALL BUNCH OF FLOWERS IS WIRED ON TO A CORD OR ROPE BASE.

are good fillers, and also poppy or other seed heads to give some texture. Choose a selection of pointed and round flower shapes and also a generous amount of good quality ribbon to tie at each end or wherever else you choose. Don't use cheap paper ribbon because this will be a permanent decoration, or one that can be used over and over again, and the paper ribbon can easily be crushed and look tatty. Anyway, if you are intending to invest so much time in making a rope why not invest a little money in some really beautiful ribbon?

Adding such bulky ingredients as cinnamon sticks, pine cones and dried fruits helps to build up the garland quickly and stops boredom setting in when you seem to have yards left to complete. Choose a selection of ingredients and make them up into bunches about 7.5 cm (3 in) long. Then wire these small bunches on to the cord base either with reel wire or individual lengths of wire. Make sure you fix the bunches on firmly so the rope is fairly safe to handle and lumps don't drop off mysteriously whenever you pick it up!

When you have finished wiring up the little bunches, which can be made up of one ingredient alone or a selection of ingredients, place the rope on a long table and look for any gaps. These can be filled easily by using my ever popular hot-glue gun and just glueing the extra pieces into position. You may say this is cheating, but because you are making something useful and not an exam piece I don't see why a good finished project can't involve a little cheating if necessary.

Fresh flower ropes

Much the same technique applies to making ropes with fresh flowers. These look wonderful twisted around pillars in churches and marquees. Try decorating staircases or fences and railings outside with them too; they make lovely talking points, and with a few pairs of willing hands (which is the best

way to tackle large flower projects as you can all work and chat at the same time) will take much less time to make than you would expect.

It is vital to make fresh flower garlands as close to the arrival of the guests as is practical. I'm not suggesting you put the final touches to your decorations as Auntie Mary comes up the drive, but don't make them up a couple of days beforehand because, being out of water, the flowers will only last a day or so. You should therefore choose flowers that last well out of water; I often use gerberas as they are large and look stunning, as well as being long-lasting. Carnations last well, as do chrysanthemums, the daisy family in general and some roses.

Try to include lots of fairly tough evergreen foliage, because it will add backbone to the rope and help to support the other ingredients. I usually choose a paper florists' ribbon as it will stand up to a little rain but is very cheap, so can be thrown away with the flowers once the occasion is over.

Combining fresh and dried ingredients
You can make up a swag that is halfway between a fresh or a dried arrangement. I often use a dried base and wire in a few fresh flowers at the last minute, then they are taken off and thrown away and the rope is stored for use another time. The base consists of glycerined leaves in various shades of green and brown, some bundles

GERBERAS ARE A GOOD CHOICE FOR FRESH FLOWER ROPES BECAUSE, IF FIRST GIVEN A GOOD DRINK OF WATER, THEY WILL LAST FOR A LONG TIME WITHOUT NEEDING FURTHER MOISTURE. HERE, THE ORANGE GERBERAS ARE INTERSPERSED WITH BUNCHES OF COW PARSLEY AND SPRIGS OF RUSCUS.

of cinnamon sticks tied with cream ribbon, which will co-ordinate with virtually any colour scheme, and some bunches of *Nigella* (love-in-a-mist) seed heads which are green and therefore also easy to blend into any colour scheme. By adding some coral ribbons and peachy 'Gerda' roses, I used it for a peach wedding. It then re-appeared with blue taffeta ribbons, delphiniums and cream roses for a summer barbecue and is about to go in the window of our shop adorned with lime green and yellow ribbons and dried flowers in shades of yellow, as an Easter decoration. At least the effort of making the basic rope seems worthwhile when it can be used over and over again.

A final alternative, if you cannot face the amount of fiddling involved with a flower rope, is to attach ribbon bows in strategic places with streamers of ribbon hanging from them, and then to attach small posies along the length of the ribbon, say every 60 cm (2 ft) or so; this saves a lot of work and makes an attractive decoration. A long table at a wedding or buffet party could have bows attached at each end and two in the middle and then flowers attached at occasional intervals along the length of the ribbons between the bows. The same idea works well on a staircase. A wide ribbon can be twisted around the banisters and then posies of flowers attached occasionally, with larger posies at the top and bottom of the stairs.

APPLES AREN'T JUST FOR EATING: THEY LOOK TERRIFIC WHEN WIRED INTO GARLANDS OR WREATHS. NO MATTER HOW PROMISING THEY LOOK, APPLES SOMETIMES HAVE THE TEXTURE OF COTTON WOOL WHICH MAKES THEM VIRTUALLY INEDIBLE, SO RATHER THAN WASTE THEM I ALWAYS TURN THEM INTO A DECORATION INSTEAD!

TOPIARY TREES

Topiary trees are not only easily made but are a lovely way to make a strong decorative statement. Two large fresh topiary trees standing outside a marquee or front door for a summer wedding look stunning and can be made up a day or two in advance, provided they are kept moist. They are relatively cheap to produce and the base can be used over and over again.

Making the base

The base is one of the most important things to get right before you start. There's no point in spending a lot of time, effort and money on ingredients, only to find that your trees blow over with the first puff of wind. I usually choose a large terracotta base, as this blends with most colour schemes and is reasonably weighty, but I always seal over any drainage holes. The stem is the next

THIS AUTUMN SWAG IS FULL OF TEXTURE AND COLOUR, THANKS TO THE WIDE VARIETY OF LEAVES, SEED PODS AND FLOWER HEADS IT CONTAINS. THESE INCLUDE *ACHILLEA* HEADS, *HELICHRYSUM*, *PHYSALIS* (CHINESE LANTERNS), DRIED POPPY HEADS, ACORNS, WHEAT EARS, OAK LEAVES, PINE CONES AND BUNDLES OF CINNAMON STICKS.

important factor. I have found most of my 'trunks' by wandering through the woods or along the beach and collecting a fallen branch or, in some cases, a very large twig. If you cannot find a piece of wood the right size you can buy dowelling from a wood yard, builders' merchant or DIY shop. Obviously this looks less interesting than a natural branch but it can be effectively camouflaged with mosses, twigs and some dark wood stain.

Having chosen your base and trunk, you need some quick-drying cement or plaster of Paris if you're making a small tree. Mix

up the cement or plaster and then place the trunk in the pot at the required angle and pour in the mixture. Do not overfill it as you will be decorating the top surface of the cement or plaster when the tree is finished. Leave the base to dry in a warm place, until you are quite certain that it is set.

Decorating the tree

If you are making a tree from fresh ingredients then you will need a ball of green florists' foam, intended for use with fresh flowers. You should choose a ball that is in proportion to the size of the base. I usually aim to make the completed ball part of the tree 1-1½ times as wide as the base, which means the foam ball should be smaller than the base to allow for the length of the material protruding from the ball. Soak the ball thoroughly in water before pushing it on to the top of the trunk; this involves a few drips as you press down on the foam, but they soon stop.

First cover the surface of the foam with a filler, usually foliage. I use ruscus, pittisporum, conifer or any other strong foliage to which I have access. Your choice of flowers will depend upon the time of year and colour scheme, but chrysanthemums and daisy sprays are available for most of the year and can be split into individual flower heads, so a little goes quite a long way. You could use many other flowers but I would not advise using luxury flowers such as lilies or orchids because they simply won't be seen to their best advantage. A topiary tree makes a strong, bold statement and so is most suitable for flowers that are long-lasting and have a good colour for your particular purpose.

A final addition can be ribbons and bows. If you are making a fresh tree, paper or florists' ribbon is useful. Instead of adding flat bows, make loops with the ribbon and wire the bottom (see diagram). The resulting bow can be pushed into the arrangement. The base also needs some attention.

THE RICH GREEN OF THE RUSCUS IN THIS FRESH TOPIARY TREE IS A DRAMATIC FOIL FOR THE DEEP PINK CHRYSANTHEMUMS AND TONING LOOPS OF RIBBON.

THIS DIAGRAM SHOWS
HOW TO WIRE UP LOOPS
OF RIBBON INTO BOWS.

DRIED TOPIARY TREES
LOOK MARVELLOUS AND
WILL LAST FOR VIRTUALLY
AS LONG AS YOU WISH
THEM TO. TO AVOID THE
TREE LOOKING BITTY,
YOU SHOULD WIRE UP
SMALL BUNCHES OF EACH
DRIED FLOWER BEFORE
INSERTING THEM IN THE
FLORAL FOAM. HERE, I
HAVE USED A MIXTURE OF
ROSE-BUDS,
HELICHRYSUM, ECHINOPS,
LAVENDER, DELPHINIUMS,
STATICE DUMOSA AND
HYDRANGEA HEADS.

Moss can look very effective, simply glued (with a hot-glue gun) on to the plaster or cement base. For a more elaborate effect you can cut out a layer of florists' foam to fit the top of the cement and then cover that with an arrangement. Alternatively, you can place a layer of foam over the cement, cover that with moss and then push the stems of a few flowers and ribbons through the moss to give a natural growing effect.

Making a dried topiary tree
I particularly love dried flower topiary trees; they look wonderful and keep for ages. They can be made in any size and suit many situations, from a bedroom to a drawing room, but of course cannot be used outside, unless it's a dry day and you keep an eye on the skies. As with fresh topiary trees, the effect needs to be bold yet simple. Miniature dried flowers can just pass unnoticed on a topiary tree so it's better to use something strong and striking. Echinops is one of my favourite tree ingredients as it has a marvellous texture, colour and shape, and the bristly globes contrast well with softer flowers such as roses or *Helichrysum.*

When making a dried flower topiary tree you need to use a grey floral foam ball designed for dried flowers, which is not soaked in water but placed on the trunk completely dry. When it is in place, cover the surface of the foam with a filler, such as *Statice dumosa,* or sea lavender as it is sometimes called. Another really lovely filler is a layer of hydrangea heads. Try to keep all the ingredients roughly the same length so that there are no straggly bits that stick out further than others.

You can incorporate many themes and ideas into a tree. If using a hydrangea base, a selection of herbs always looks and smells wonderful. When you are using quite fine items like dried herbs, they should be wired into bunches before being pushed into the foam; fairly large clusters of such herbs as marjoram or sage look far more effective than occasional stems dotted here and there around an arrangement.

Spices such as ginger root, cinnamon sticks and dried chilli peppers can all look effective in a design. A Christmas tree could be made from spruce or conifer branches, and decorated with spices and ribbons. Subtle pastel colour schemes look very beautiful in bedrooms and bathrooms, but if your bathroom gets very steamy the humid atmosphere can affect the flowers. Special dried flower trees can be made for weddings, using groups of peach roses, cream and champagne roses, mixed with apricot statice and *Helichrysum*, cream peonies and satin ribbons. Golden and silver weddings can also be celebrated with trees with suitable colour schemes; steely blues, grey and silver for a silver wedding tree and a stunning range of natural old golds and creams for a golden wedding.

A small tree could be made for the arrival of a new baby, and it would make an unusual gift. For a baby girl you could make a small tree with pink rose-buds and pink ribbons, or blue larkspur and delphiniums with cream rose-buds for a boy. Obviously the tree would have to be removed from the nursery once the child was able to crawl, in case he or she wanted to eat it, but the mother would be able to enjoy the tree for about a year before that happened.

DECORATING THE TABLE
Flowers can decorate a kitchen or dining table in all sorts of ways. Whether the occasion you are planning is a large formal wedding, banquet, elegant dinner party or a small family meal, there are plenty of simple but effective ideas that look good and take little time.

Using pots of plants
Complicated flower arrangements are not the only way to create pretty effects. As most of us can't spare much time to prepare for an average dinner party, flowers often

have to take second place to making sure the guests have something to eat! Potted plants in flower can be a very useful stand-by at those times; groups of African violets, azaleas or even miniature roses can make a lovely display. Depending on the size of the individual plants and their pots, I would suggest using a group of two or three, which can be arranged in a circular or oval dish, according to the shape of the table. Pack the spaces between the pots, and cover the pots themselves, with mosses to give a more natural effect. You can also incorporate candles into this arrangement, but do make sure you keep the flames away from any flowers or foliage that could catch fire.

For tables with a Christmas theme, you could arrange some pots of poinsettias or ivies with elegant ivory candles, which could be lit or not depending on the height of the plants. Many different potted plants lend themselves to this treatment. For example, a summer supper could have a collection of potted herbs in the middle of the table, while an autumn dinner could have pots of bronze, red and gold chrysanthemums.

IF YOU ARE SHORT OF TIME – AND WHO ISN'T – WHEN PREPARING A SPECIAL MEAL, YOU CAN MAKE A TABLE ARRANGEMENT IN MINUTES WITH THE HELP OF SOME CANDLES, A FEW PLANTS AND SOME MOSS. I USED AZALEAS FOR THIS ARRANGEMENT, BUT YOU COULD USE WHATEVER YOU HAD TO HAND: PERHAPS POTS OF GERANIUMS IN THE SUMMER OR AFRICAN VIOLETS IN THE WINTER.

Driftwood arrangements

If you want to spend a little more time and effort on a table arrangement, a collection of driftwood can be very useful. Arrange your driftwood in a formation that echoes the shape of the table, leaving random holes and gaps to fill with flowers. You can use dried or fresh flowers but I find it is quicker to work with fresh flowers when using driftwood. Take some green florists' foam for fresh arrangements and soak it well in water. Cut some pieces to fit the gaps you have left within the driftwood arrangement and cover each piece with strong clingfilm. These pieces of foam can now sit on a polished surface without damaging it. If, however, the surface is too precious to risk even that, you should place some extra base material, such as a wooden board or large sheet of

THIS DRIFTWOOD ARRANGEMENT, CONTAINING DWARF NARCISSI, SNAKE'S HEAD FRITILLARIES AND SPRIGS OF HEATHER, WOULD BE A MARVELLOUS CENTREPIECE FOR AN EASTER LUNCH PARTY.

polythene, under the entire arrangement.

Choose your selection of flowers and insert them in the foam carefully, using a skewer to make the preliminary hole in the clingfilm. Once you have a few flowers in each gap – don't overfill the arrangement or it will stop looking natural – you can camouflage the pieces of foam, and any other gaps, with plenty of moss.

Although I have illustrated this idea with a mixture of spring flowers, you could easily make a similar arrangement with autumn leaves and flowers in shades of red and bronze. For a Christmas arrangement you could spray some 'snow' on to the moss. High summer is easy because of the number of fresh flowers available but you could also add a few shells or other accessories that took your fancy.

Individual arrangements

One of the problems with a central table arrangement is that, if you are already short of space, it clutters up the table even more. I like to put bowls of vegetables in the middle of my table so everyone can reach them, so I prefer to give each person an individual arrangement. You can collect a few flowers from the garden and put them in a tiny vase at each place setting. Alternatively, if you don't have a large enough supply of small vases, you could make miniature posies of flowers. These only take a few minutes to put together yet are often taken home and treasured by the guests.

Here I have made up bunches of snowdrops and variegated ivy leaves, tied with white ribbon. Violets and other diminutive flowers also look good like this. Alternatively you could pick small bunches of fresh herbs and tie them with pretty ribbons or just use a miscellany of flowers and herbs picked at random from the garden. Don't be tempted to use too many flowers for each person; you only need a small bunch, mixed with a couple of pieces of foliage, to give a pretty but natural effect.

When flowers are scarce in the garden you can make lovely posies from berries, clematis seed heads, sprigs of evergreen foliage and other odds and ends. The ribbon is important; you only need a small length so treat yourself to a really lovely piece of satin or taffeta ribbon that will set off the flowers beautifully. A cheap scrap of ribbon will detract from the flowers and look awful. I keep a good supply of pale shades of very narrow baby ribbon, which is quite cheap to buy and can be tied around little bunches, using one or two colours at a time. A small posy of flowers laid on a side plate looks charming and is an immediate talking point. Tying the posies with some lace looks lovely in the right setting, so use your imagination.

If you need something even easier than tying a ribbon around a small posy of flowers, you can tuck a couple of flowers and leaves

into a napkin ring. This, of course, assumes that you are using linen napkins and pretty napkin rings. I use linen napkins for very special occasions and am lucky enough to own some beautiful family silver napkin rings. However, I must admit that they only come out on high days and holidays because cleaning silver is one of my least favourite jobs!

I ENJOY MAKING UP TINY POSIES TO PUT BY EACH GUEST'S PLATE, AND IT'S AN EASY IDEA TO COPY. DO REMEMBER, HOWEVER, TO USE ONLY TINY FLOWERS: ANYTHING TOO LARGE WILL LOOK QUITE WRONG AND SPOIL THE SCALE.

old-fashioned roses look lovely used by themselves), or whatever else you have in the garden. Thread them carefully through the napkin ring and add a couple of leaves. That is easy enough for anyone to do and it looks charming. The only drawback is when an over-conscientious 'helpful' guest insists on getting up and collecting all the flowers to put them in water straightaway so they don't wilt – it spoils the effect!

LARGER POSIES AND BOUQUETS

Although bottles of wine are always appreciated as a gift for the host and hostess, it is much nicer to take something a little less predictable. Flowers always please, and if you can put a little extra effort into their presentation they will look extra special. The glamour and glitz of a florists' wrapped bouquet is too impersonal a touch when you're visiting friends for dinner; it's nicer and much prettier if you can pick a bunch of flowers from your garden. If you don't have a garden, then choose a collection of flowers from the florist in a colour scheme that you think may blend with your hosts' decor. It is easy to arrange the flowers into an informal posy tied with a ribbon.

Making up a bunch of flowers

Lay the flowers carefully on a wipeable surface, because they will drip water while you are arranging them. Place some long flowers at the back of the bunch and then carefully layer the flowers so they are shown to their best advantage. Make sure that all the stalks reach at least to the point where you will be tying the bow. If you want to secure the bunch first you can wind some florists' wire around that point, or just tie it firmly with a piece of ribbon. When your hostess receives the gift she only has to untie the ribbon to put all the flowers in water, ready arranged.

This sort of really informal bunch looks stunning with a mixed selection of flowers or one type of flower in one or many colours.

HERE IS ANOTHER IDEA FOR INDIVIDUAL TABLE ARRANGEMENTS. THESE NAPKIN RINGS HAVE BEEN DECORATED WITH A FEW *MUSCARI*, SPRIGS OF VARIEGATED IVY AND RUE LEAVES. THE ONLY DRAWBACK IS THAT IT SEEMS A SHAME TO USE THE NAPKIN AND DISMANTLE SUCH A PRETTY ARRANGEMENT!

The beautiful napkin rings in the photograph above belong to a friend, and I think their greeny verdigris finish gives them an immediate charm. A regular stroll around antique or junk shops can often unearth lovely treasures and they need not cost the earth. I must say that whenever I suggest the family should come with me around antique shops there are general groans and cries of 'Hide the cheque book'. I can't think why!

Take a couple of flowers, such as anemones, *Muscari* or roses (the large

IT'S ALWAYS LOVELY TO BE
GIVEN FLOWERS, BUT HOW
MUCH NICER TO RECEIVE A
BUNCH THAT HAVE
ALREADY BEEN
ARRANGED, SO ALL YOU
NEED DO IS PUT THEM IN A
VASE OF WATER.

Tussie-mussies and posies

You could also make a slightly more complicated posy or tussie-mussie to take as a gift. These circular posies can be made with or without a frill of starched cotton or lace at the back of the posy. Originally these nosegays or posies were used to convey messages as well as ward off unpleasant smells, so you could easily incorporate the language of flowers into such a posy as an added feature.

The centrepiece of the arrangement should be a lovely rose or other fairly large flower, which can then be surrounded by a circle of another sort of flower, such as lavender, gypsophila, solidaster or fresh herbs. More rings can then be added, each circle being wrapped with lightweight florists' wire to bind it in position. If you are using a frill to finish the bouquet you can use a fairly solid item for the last ring; if you want to omit the frill then choose a light airy ingredient to finish the pattern. *Alchemilla mollis* is very effective and dill or cow parsley would look wonderful.

LILIES ARE AMONG THE CLASSIC WEDDING FLOWERS, AND THEIR SCENT IS QUITE HEAVENLY. THIS SORT OF LOOSE BUNCH IS EASILY ASSEMBLED, BUT DO MAKE SURE THE STEMS ARE TIED FIRMLY TOGETHER.

SIMPLE BRIDAL FLOWERS

Although many brides long for a formal service with white fairytale gowns and all the trimmings, there is a growing number of couples who want a simple family ceremony at home surrounded by friends but without the massive cost of an elaborate wedding. The bride's family can also gain much satisfaction from their involvement in making the day really special. Although the idea of catering or doing the flowers for a wedding may terrify some people it will certainly appeal to many others.

Wedding flowers can be very simple but effective, provided you have given some thought and planning to the colour scheme, the flowers available at that time of year and the number of helpers available. Many flower-minded friends and neighbours would love to be asked to help with a wedding, and will gladly give hours of their time and enjoy being involved in such a happy and joyous occasion.

Fresh topiary trees are easy to make slightly ahead of time and look stunning flanking doorways or entrances to a marquee. Ropes of flowers twined around pillars or gateways also look very beautiful, but most important of all are the bridal party flowers. Many people may think they couldn't cope with making a bridal bouquet, but really it depends on the style that is required. If you want a very formal, traditional bouquet it may be wiser to involve a local florist, but if something more informal and countrified could fit the bill you might easily be able to make it yourself. The flowers used in the photograph on the left are a mixture of lilies and winter jasmine, but you could just as easily use a selection of roses with some gypsophila, or any other simple combination that appeals. The flowers were arranged in the same way as for the informal posy. When making a bridal bouquet, make sure the stalks all come past the point at which you want to tie the bunch together, and then secure it with wires and ribbon. For a less

WORKING WITH DRIED
FLOWERS FOR A WEDDING
IS A JOY TO ME BECAUSE
THERE IS NO LAST-MINUTE
RUSH OR PANIC TO
CONTEND WITH.

special occasion you can just use ribbon, but I would suggest being safe rather than sorry when making wedding flowers!

Even the more traditional style of bouquet has become much easier to make now that foam bouquet holders are available; it is just like making a small flower arrangement on a skipping rope handle. These bouquet bases are available from a few garden centres, florists' shops and some mail order craft suppliers. I have sold many such bases to brides' mothers and they have all said that they felt very proud of their achievement when they saw the photographs.

So many people have attended my wedding flowers courses convinced that that they wouldn't be able to cope, yet have gone away realizing that they not only have more creative ability than they thought but also feel confident about trying to arrange all the flowers for a forthcoming wedding. You must have a little courage and faith in your abilities for the best results.

I went to a wedding last summer where the bride carried a large tied bunch of Queen Anne's lace, or cow parsley, and large white daisies. It looked very lovely and will be remembered for many years for its simplicity and beauty.

Dried wedding flowers

The only drawback to tackling the flowers for a wedding is the last-minute nature of the project, but even this can be completely overcome if you choose dried flowers. I should admit to a strong bias here as I love really beautiful dried flowers. I agree there are many second-rate dried flower arrangements on the market, but there are many sources of really first-class flowers and finished arrangements. If you opt for dried flowers, your planning can begin many weeks, or even months, in advance. However, if you are making up arrangements or bouquets many months in advance, do remember that the flowers must be kept in

FACING PAGE: THIS FRESH
HERBAL WREATH
INCLUDES BUNCHES OF
PARSLEY, SAGE, BORAGE,
CHERVIL, THYME, BAY,
ROSEMARY AND BASIL.
THE HERBS CAN EITHER
BE USED FRESH OR LEFT
TO DRY ON THE WREATH.

BELOW: IF YOU HAVE
PICKED TOO MANY HERBS
FOR USE IN A WREATH AND
HAVE SOME LEFT OVER,
YOU CAN DRY THEM FOR
USE LATER. TO DO THIS,
TIE THEM IN SMALL
BUNCHES AND LEAVE ON A
WIRE CAKE RACK IN A
COOL, DARK PLACE FOR A
COUPLE OF WEEKS UNTIL
COMPLETELY DRY.

the dark, completely dry and away from possible attacks from our rodent and insect friends. It wouldn't be the same, somehow, walking up the aisle carrying a harvest mouse asleep in your bouquet. Actually, knowing my daughter, she would love it!

When working with dried flowers for a wedding it helps to choose large-headed flowers like peonies or roses, as they make a stronger statement and look extremely elegant. The head-dress and bouquet in the photograph on page 133 were made from peonies, *Milium paniculatum* or millet, which has a soft feathery effect, some glycerined beech leaves, silver rose *Helichrysum* and soft green oregano. I also added some touches of glycerined gypsophila that had been coloured grey.

The bouquet is simple to make, using one of the foam bouquet bases that I mentioned earlier. The flowers are simply inserted as they would be in a fresh foam-based arrangement. The head-dress may be slightly more difficult to make, but with a little practice can look very professional. The plant material is first wired into small mixed bunches and then wired on to a wire circle covered with green florists' tape. If there are any glaring gaps when you have

finished, extra leaves or flowers can be glued on with a hot-glue gun to even out any problem areas.

One of the extra bonuses of dried flower bouquets is that you can keep them. I have one I made many years ago which has been kept in a special hand-painted hat box, where I keep my special treasures. Because it has been kept warm and in the dark it still looks lovely. You could also keep the flowers on a dressing table but don't expect them to keep their colours for so long if they are exposed to the light.

DECORATING WITH HERBS

Herbs are one of my favourite groups of plants; whether I use them fresh or dried, for cooking or for decoration, they always please me. Since becoming more interested in herbs and their uses in the last few years, I have found tremendous pleasure in growing and using them. It really is worth growing some plants in the garden or on the kitchen window-sill, because, for culinary purposes, nothing compares to the magic of fresh herbs. Dried herbs are only used in an emergency now that I have been so totally converted to the far more subtle flavours and delicious tastes of fresh herbs. Another bonus is that if you are growing your own herbs you can dry some for decorative use as well.

Herbal wreaths make lovely presents and if you are feeling selfish, they also make lovely presents for yourself! You can make them just as easily from fresh herbs or dried. In both cases I use a hot-glue gun (I think I should buy shares in the company) but you could also wire the small bunches on to a wreath base if you preferred.

Fresh herbal wreaths

The fresh herb wreath in the picture on the facing page was made after wandering along the paths of my little herb garden and choosing different colours and shapes that appealed to me. I then wired them into

small bunches and glued them into a spiral pattern around the wreath base. As this particular wreath base is fairly wide it took quite a reasonable quantity of herbs, but it makes a lovely decoration for the kitchen. You can just snip off a small amount to use in cooking, either when the herbs are fresh or later when they have dried, and then fill the gap with another bunch of the same or a slightly different herb. This way the wreath is always changing and evolving. At one point I added a lot more of the purple basil, just because I love the colour so much, and as I used it the wreath turned a pale green with more thyme and sage. Once you have the wreath base and a glue gun it really doesn't take very long to make the wreath and it is a very pretty present for anyone who loves their garden or kitchen.

I LOVE MAKING WREATHS FROM DRIED HERBS: THERE ARE SO MANY DIFFERENT COLOURS, SHAPES AND TEXTURES TO CHOOSE FROM THAT THE VARIATIONS ARE ENDLESS. THEY ALSO LOOK TERRIFIC HANGING ON THE KITCHEN WALL.

Dried herbal wreaths
The dried flower wreath has a slightly different base – a heart shape made from willow tree trimmings in the spring. I wind these twigs around a heart-shaped block, and they are then held in place with wires around the wreath. It has to be left on the block to dry or it collapses out of shape. The herbs can be added when it has dried, using a hot-glue gun. Here the herbs have been mixed with heather and lavender to give a bolder and stronger colour.

Dried herbs and flowers have also been used to decorate a straw plait. In this case I bought the plait ready-made, but you could easily make one yourself from straw, raffia or any other natural twine. This plait is decorated with marjoram and peach roses, attached with glue in a spiral design that makes it seem as if the dried herbs will twist behind the plait. Marjoram is one of my favourite dried herbs as it has such a good striking colour and gentle form, and I use it a great deal, especially with roses.

CHRISTMAS
Christmas is a time when many of us decorate our homes, but the best decorations are those that the family has made together rather than the commercially available varieties. I love seeing family homes decorated with paper chains made by the children, or a tree that is obviously laden with treasured family decorations rather than one that is beautifully colour co-ordinated. One of the most exciting parts of Christmas for me is opening the Christmas tree decoration box and bringing out our treats and surprises that have been loved for many years. We have a doll called Sylvia, who belongs on the top of the tree. She was bought for a very small sum about sixty years ago and has really beautiful teeth and a porcelain face and hands. We often give her a new Christmas outfit or a new wand but she is still one of the centrepieces of our family Christmas.

THE COLOURS IN THIS
HERBAL PLAIT ARE
STUNNING: I LOVE THE
COMBINATION OF THE
DRIED LAVENDER,
MARJORAM AND PEACH
ROSES, AND IT SMELLS
GOOD, TOO!

WHY SHOULDN'T BIRDS HAVE THEIR OWN CHRISTMAS TREE? IT MAKES A HIGHLY DECORATIVE CHANGE FROM SCATTERING FOOD ON A BIRD TABLE OR OVER THE GRASS, AND PROVIDES HOURS OF ENTERTAINMENT TOO, AS THE BIRDS SCRABBLE FOR SPACE ON THE BRANCHES. DON'T FORGET TO ADD MORE FOOD WHEN THE EXISTING GOODIES HAVE BEEN EATEN.

Every year new tree decorations join the collection to be admired for many years to come, and every year we make a few extra decorations to fill up the tree – I think by the year 2000 we may need two trees! Simple decorations like bundles of cinnamon sticks or lavender tied with gold cord look very attractive, and we added miniature parcels last year, wrapped in a tartan fabric with gold cord tassels.

Popcorn garlands

One fun addition to the tree that can be made by all the family is a popcorn garland. Popcorn is easy to thread and it's nice to eat the remains. However, our family seem unable to differentiate between the remains and those that are meant to be threaded on to the strings, so buy extra just in case! The popcorn is a lot easier to handle if you leave it for a couple of days to get stale (proportionately less gets eaten, as well) then, using a strong but fairly fine thread and long needles, get stringing. One other point – do make sure there is a substantial knot at one end of the string or the popcorn will pass down the string and form a separate pile on the kitchen table. I know because this happened to some early strings we were making. It caused much hilarity but wasted rather a lot of time!

Feeding the birds

While you are decorating your tree and planning the scrumptious goodies you will be eating over the Christmas period, please don't forget the birds. Winter can be hard for them, according to the strength of the frosts and snow, so why not make a separate Christmas tree especially for the birds? You can either buy one specially or use a suitable tree or shrub already growing in the garden. Tie a collection of small bundles of crusts, bacon rinds, nuts and chains of peanuts in their shells all over the tree, then sit inside and watch. The antics of the birds grabbing their Christmas present can keep you amused for hours.

Festive fragrances

This festive time of year is usually a busy one for entertaining, so you will probably want to make sure that the house smells welcoming and festive. I usually make a big bowl of Christmas pot-pourri to sit in the drawing room or hall. There are lots of Christmassy ingredients that you can use; I concentrate on spices and pine cones but you could add holly or mistletoe if you liked. Once you have made your own pot-pourri a few times, the bug will grab you, because what started as an innocent hobby for me has become an overpowering obsession. Whenever I see an ingredient that could be used in pot-pourri I dry or preserve it by the sackful and am constantly experimenting with new and different oils.

CHRISTMAS POT-POURRI

I use a 600 ml (1 pint) glass kitchen measuring jug as my basic measure and fill it, then level off the top.

10 measures spruce needles	5 measures tiny cones
5 measures dried root ginger	150-175 g (5-6 oz) calamus root or cut orris root
10 measures small to medium pine cones	12 ml (½ fl oz) Country Christmas oil
1 large bundle of cinnamon sticks (about 18-20 sticks)	

Using a large coffee jar or similar, pour in the calamus or orris root and add the oil.

Shake well, ensuring all the oil is absorbed, then leave the mixture for a couple of days, shaking it occasionally whenever you pass by.

Reserve some of the cinnamon sticks for decorating the top of the pot-pourri, then break the remaining sticks into three. Mix all the ingredients in a large mixing bowl and add the root and oil mixture. I suggest using a couple of metal spoons so you don't have to touch the pot-pourri with your hands, because the oil does make them smell for some time. Once the ingredients are well mixed, leave them in a large, sealed, plastic bag for a couple of weeks, shaking it regularly. The pot-pourri will then be ready.

If you cannot buy a suitable ready-mixed oil then try mixing pine essential oil with a little orange, lemon and cinnamon oils.

CHOOSE THE LARGEST BOWL YOU CAN FIND TO DISPLAY THIS CHRISTMAS POT-POURRI, SO ALL THE INGREDIENTS CAN BE VIEWED TO THEIR BEST ADVANTAGE.

Decorating Bedrooms

If you are having guests to stay it's always welcoming for them to see a vase of flowers or decoration in their bedroom. There has to be a limit to the size and scale of any arrangement for a bedroom, because too many overpowering flowers can cause a restless night, especially for a hay fever sufferer, but it does look lovely.

Gently perfumed flowers make the bedroom smell lovely, but beware of anything too overpoweringly fragrant. If you are lucky enough to have a large, spacious bedroom then a suitably large arrangement of flowers would look great. If, however, you have a reasonably sized room you shouldn't make anything too big.

A dainty arrangement by the bedside always looks charming, and on the left I have used anemones and primulas. I always find flowers picked from the garden most homely and welcoming, but you could make an equally beautiful arrangement with rosebuds or freesias from the florist.

Herbal pillows

As well as decorating the bedroom with flowers you could also make your guests feel especially welcome by placing sweet-smelling herbal pillows on their beds. Hops have long been renowned for their sleep-inducing properties and can be slipped inside a pillow in a muslin case. One of the nicest ways of using herbs, I think, is to make a small muslin pillow, about 20 × 15 cm (8 × 6 in), and to fill it with herbs, keeping it fairly flat. Then it can be slipped inside an existing cushion or pillow on the bed to exude its sweet smell. Do check before you put herbs into a guest's pillow that he or she is not sensitive to them: how awful to have someone sneezing all night because you hadn't explained where the herbal sachet was hidden.

Herbal sachets can also be slipped inside cushions in the drawing room. The movement of people sitting on the cushions and bruising the herbs helps to release their fragrance.

FACING PAGE: BEDSIDE TABLE ARRANGEMENTS CAN VARY IN SIZE FROM TINY TO LARGE, ACCORDING TO THE SIZE OF THE BEDROOM. ABOVE: CUSHIONS FILLED WITH HERBAL SACHETS SMELL DELECTABLE.

INDEX

ACKNOWLEDGEMENTS

I should like to thank a great many people for their help with this book, but for reasons of space I must restrict myself to a few key people. Jane Struthers, the project editor on this book, has been so diplomatic and helpful that I'm sure we would all have had nervous breakdowns without her. Debbie Patterson rates as one of the most professional and gifted photographers that I have ever worked with, and we had a good time along the way. My thanks to everyone at Letts, especially Cortina Butler for her faith in me, and Gary Chapman for his help with the cakes and for being fun to be around.

Thanks to Gill Beanland and Marion Spencer for their help with the dried flowers; Mandy Holmes for making the sachets; Diana Hatherly for her help with the cookery in Devon and Meg Jansz for tackling most of the remaining recipes. Thanks to the testing ground for Suttons Seeds, who kindly gave the pumpkins for the Harvest and Thanksgiving chapter. Thanks to Steven Stellingwerf for his work on the cakes and Lucy Mason for her help with the photography. Finally, I should like to extend grateful thanks to everyone who has been on one of my courses and acted as a guinea pig when I have tested these recipes at lunch times or in the evenings.

Debbie Patterson would like to thank:

Perfect Glass
5 Park Walk
London SW10

Manic Botanic
2 Silver Place
London W1

Gallery of Antique Costumes and Textiles
2 Church Street
London NW8

SUPPLIERS

For dried flowers by mail order:

The Hop Shop
Castle Farm
Shoreham
Sevenoaks
Kent
Telephone: (09592) 3219

For details of courses on
dried flowers, pressed flowers,
herbs and pot-pourri making:

Joanna Sheen Limited (Courses)
PO Box 52
Newton Abbot
South Devon
Telephone: (0626) 872405,
9.30 a.m. – 5.00 p.m. weekdays only

For pot-pourri ingredients
and oils, pressed flower and
dried flower components,
baskets and other accessories:

Joanna Sheen Limited
7 Lucius Street
Torquay
South Devon
Telephone: (0803) 201311

Shop open 9 a.m. – 5.30 p.m.
Monday to Friday (closed for
lunch between 1–2 p.m.)